WEIRD SH!T

Summersdale Publishers Ltd
46 West Street
Chichester
West Sussex
PO19 1RP
UK

www.summersdale.com

Printed and bound in the Czech Republic

ISBN: 978-1-84953-541-0

Substantial discounts on bulk quantities of Summersdale books are available to corporations, professional associations and other organisations. For details contact Nicky Douglas by telephone: +44 (0) 1243 756902, fax: +44 (0) 1243 786300 or email: nicky@summersdale.com.

WEIRD SH!T

TRUE STORIES TO SHOCK, STUN, ASTOUND AND AMAZE

MARK LEIGH

summersdale

DISCLAIMER

ABOUT THE AUTHOR

Mark Leigh has been called the Sultan of Strange, the Prince of the Peculiar and the King of the Bizarre (the latter by someone who didn't quite understand the concept of alliteration). He has dedicated a large part of his life to researching and cataloguing curiosities and oddities in the world around us; however critics have commented that he really should get out more.

Despite immersing himself in *Weird Sh!t*, Mark has somehow found time to write and co-write forty-nine humour and trivia books on subjects as diverse as celebrities, extra-terrestrials, swearing pets and toilets.

Mark lives in Surrey with his family and dog. When he's not writing, Mark steals pens and photocopier paper from his job at a marketing agency.

For more details visit **www.mark-leigh.com**

CONTENTS

INTRODUCTION

We are all a little weird and life is a little weird...

Dr Seuss

Shit isn't the only thing that happens.

Weird shit happens.

And it's far more common than you might imagine.

In the course of researching this book I've come across weird shit from way back in the day, like the Roman emperor who would stand naked in the doorway of his palace bedroom making advances at his elite guard, right up to the present, such as the Death Row prisoner who consumed a whopping 29,000 calories in his last meal.

Weird shit lies bubbling under the surface, biding its time, just waiting for that perfect moment to strike, reminding us that things are never as normal as they might seem. No one is immune from weird shit. It can just as easily involve the man or woman in the street, like the Chinese girl who lives a normal life even though she was born with her feet facing backwards, as it can the rich and famous – for example, Salvador Dalí wearing a home-made cologne made of fish glue and goat manure. Weird shit even affects royalty, like King Charles VI of France who refused to travel by coach because he believed his legs were made of glass and they might shatter.

But remember, no matter how outrageous or bizarre it may sound, all the weird shit in this book has been reported as true. Like the inventor of Pringles being cremated and having his ashes buried in a Pringles can, the mass murderer who auditioned for a boy band, or the Japanese department store that caused great offence after they managed to confuse Santa Claus with Jesus Christ.

So, kick back, raise your eyebrows, suspend your disbelief and utter 'WTF!'

You couldn't make it up if you tried.

Mark Leigh
Surrey, England 2014

ANIMAL TALES

A man in San Francisco brought the proliferation of dog droppings on the city's streets to the notice of the authorities in a way that only a San Franciscan could. He garnished every pile he came across with whipped cream and a maraschino cherry.

Bruno Alti of Milan thought he had a bargain after buying a puppy from a stranger for the equivalent of about £30. The dog refused to bark and at times would hiss and behave in a quite menacing manner.
A visit to his local vet confirmed that Mr Alti had in fact bought a lion cub.

A barnacle has the largest penis of any animal in relation to its size.

In 1954 a herd of elephants was devouring a sugar-cane crop in Terai, India, so villagers set a hedge alight to scare them away. This seemed to do the trick until the elephants returned after visiting a nearby stream, put out the fire with their trunks, and continued with their feast.

A chameleon's tongue can be up to twice as long as its body and head combined, and can shoot out as fast as sixteen feet per second.

Madonna was reported to have sent her pet chihuahua, Chiquita, for therapy after she thought it was depressed over the attention being given to her new baby Lourdes.

Cattle can be identified by their nose prints, just as humans can be identified by their fingerprints.

Llamas are born with an extra pair of fighting teeth that they can use to bite off other llamas' testicles in order to make them the only fertile male in their group.

Bengal villagers who are frightened of being attacked by tigers have started wearing human masks on the back of their heads. Tigers will only ever attack from behind and apparently can't work out what to do when confronted with a human with two faces.

One of the most popular attractions in the fete held in Curwensville, Pennsylvania, consists of an eight-foot cage filled with rattlesnakes. Entrants go into the cage and try to put five of the snakes into a sack in the fastest time. To encourage safe handling of the rattlesnakes, anyone that gets bitten receives a time penalty.

The armadillo is the only creature apart from humans that can get leprosy.

Yak's milk is pink.

A researcher from Cambridge University, who'd been studying the mating habits of penguins for five years, observed that some female penguins were willing to offer sex to male penguins who were not their mates in return for help moving nest-building stones. The actions of these 'penguin prostitutes' are thought to be unique among animals.

The typical laboratory mouse runs on average five miles per day on its exercise wheel.

Christmas Day 1982 was not a joyous occasion for Claudette Reinert; she sustained serious injuries when her poodle accidentally pushed her out of her fourth-floor Strasbourg apartment. As she was getting ready to take her dog out for a walk, it became overexcited and jumped up, knocking her through an open window.

There are one million ants for every human in the world.

A Masai tribesman was arrested in February 1983 for attacking a lion in Nairobi, Kenya. He explained that his brother had been killed by a lion and he was exacting his revenge. The tribesman had thrown himself at the lion and began strangling it before he was pulled off by guards. The lion in question was a stuffed one that resided in the lobby of the Nairobi Ministry of Tourism. After his arrest he stated that he had had no idea that the lion was stuffed; he'd just assumed it was very docile.

An ostrich's eye is bigger than its brain.

Bears in North America have been known to climb telegraph poles in search of honey. The humming of the wires makes them think that beehives are at the very top.

Grasshoppers who ingest the leaves of wild marijuana plants have been found to jump abnormally high... even for a grasshopper.

In order to protect themselves, some creatures never go to sleep entirely; while one half of their brain goes to sleep, the other half remains alert. This manifests itself in sleeping with one eye open. Creatures who display this peculiarity include porpoises, some species of whale, dolphin and seal, the domestic chicken, the common blackbird, the mallard and the peregrine falcon.

The elephant is the only mammal that can't jump.

Caterpillars were responsible for the derailment of a goods train in the central Italian town of Fabriano in June 1982. The train hit a procession of them almost two miles long and thirty-three feet wide as it crossed the tracks; the wheels lost traction and the train jumped the rails.

You'll die if you eat a whole polar bear. Our bodies couldn't cope with the huge amount of vitamin A stored in its liver.

A man from Silver Spring in Maryland was infected by rabies after having sex with a raccoon. He was charged with animal cruelty but was acquitted after he pointed out that the raccoon was actually dead at the time.

From 1981 to 1994 the mayor of Sunol, a small town in California, was an 85-lb part-Labrador part-Rottweiler called Bosco. He led the town parade every year, wearing a red satin bow around his neck. His popularity among the 1,500 population had grown every year since his campaign manager had declared a three-point manifesto: 'A cat in every tree, a bone in every dish and a fire hydrant on every street corner.'

The small mountain town of Guffey in Colorado has had a succession of feline mayors. This began in 1988 with a cat named Paisley. It was followed by Smudge le Plume (killed by an owl while in office), Whiffey le Gone, and Monster, which lived at the back of a garage during its spell in office.

The Texas horned lizard (the official state reptile) can increase the blood pressure in its head to such a degree that it can squirt blood out of its eye into the face of predators from as far away as five feet.

A blue whale is about 25 feet long at birth.

Man poisons snake! It happened in India in 1981 when a venomous snake bit a drug addict while he slept. The man survived but the snake, having absorbed toxins from the man's blood, was found dead.

Abting Bangat, a fifteen-year-old Filipino boy, was swallowed whole by a python that he disturbed when exploring a cave near his home in 1983. Other members of his tribe searching for him found the snake and killed it but on slicing it open, found that Abting was already dead.

A budgie that escaped from its cage in Nottingham in August 1982 was returned home safe and sound shortly afterwards after being found by a local schoolboy. The budgie had told the boy his name and address.

Scientific studies have shown that mosquitoes are more likely to bite blondes but the reason isn't down to any personal preference for hair types. The simple reason is that the insects are known to have poor eyesight and find it easier to pick out light colours against dark backgrounds.

Studies have shown that some cats get sexually aroused when they are spanked.

Castrated dogs can regain some of their lost manhood (doghood?) by the addition of plastic testicle implants called neuticles. According to the inventor, these help the dog regain his self-esteem by making him appear the same as his non-neutered buddies.

When Cuba suffered widespread food shortages in 1994, the country's cat population fell by 400,000.

CALL A DOCTOR!

In 1953 Mrs Alice Coe visited her aunt in a psychiatric hospital in Jamestown, Virginia, only to find she'd just passed peacefully away. Feeling tired while she gathered her dead aunt's possessions together, Mrs Coe got into her bed for a nap. Awoken by a doctor telling her that she was being transferred to a new room, Mrs Coe obediently went with him and stayed in the hospital for twenty-five years, until the case of mistaken identity was finally spotted in 1978.

Wim Hof of the Netherlands (nicknamed the Iceman) is totally immune to the cold and has climbed Mont Blanc wearing just shoes and shorts.

Villagers living in an isolated mountain district in the Dominican Republic suffer from an inherited enzyme deficiency that has the effect of making some of the males develop initially as females. They are born with female genitalia and body shapes until puberty, at which point they develop penises, their testicles drop and their voices break. Known as machihembras, the boys are brought up as girls until the 'change' and apparently easily adjust to their new sexual identity thereafter.

Charles Osborne (1894–1991) of Iowa had the hiccups non-stop for almost sixty-eight years, from 1922 until 1990. It started while he was weighing a hog on his farm. Trying to lift the 159-kg (350-lb) animal, he slipped and, according to a later diagnosis, ruptured a tiny blood vessel in his brain that inhibits the hiccup response. Osborne started hiccupping at a rate of about forty per minute but this slowed in later life to a mere twenty. After hiccupping an estimated 430 million times, the hiccupping mysteriously stopped a year before his death.

If the lining of mucus were to disappear from your stomach, your stomach would digest itself.

According to the *Bangkok Post* at least a hundred men in Thailand underwent penis-enlargement operations performed by bogus doctors. The paper reported that the men's penises were injected with a mixture of olive oil, chalk and other unknown substances to provide bulk. An official at a hospital in Chiang Mai was reported to say, 'I've even seen penises containing bits of the Bangkok telephone directory.'

The youngest authenticated person to give birth was Lina Medina, who was born in 1933 in Ticrapo, Peru. When she was aged five, her mother took her to the local hospital worried that her daughter's stomach was steadily increasing in size. There, Dr Gerardo Lozada diagnosed that Lina was pregnant and, six weeks after his diagnosis, on 14 May 1939, she gave birth via Caesarean section to a baby boy. Lina was able to become pregnant at such a young age due to a very rare condition known as 'precocious puberty' – an extremely early onset of sexual development. Despite investigations by the authorities, it was never discovered how Lina became pregnant or who the father was.

As with fingerprints, every person has a unique tongue print.

In 1997 the Malaysian Minister of Culture, Arts and Tourism suggested a way to encourage more visitors to the country – by holding mass public circumcisions. He told the *Daily Star* newspaper that it offered tourists 'something different from the norm'.

A man visiting his brother who was a patient in a psychiatric hospital in Wellington, New Zealand, was himself detained for a psychological evaluation. He'd driven his car up the hospital steps and parked it in the ward.

The presence of additional breasts is a condition known as polymastia; it's a form of atavism, an evolutionary throwback. In 1886, a Professor Neugenbauer presented to the French Academy of Medicine a woman with ten individual lactating breasts. Three months later, Dr P. J. Stoyanoff exhibited a twenty-three-year-old Polish woman who also had eight additional breasts, all of which secreted milk.

Dr Ari Roga was a successful physician in Salzburg, Austria, with a penchant for baking fancy decorated cakes for his patients. When one of them commented that he must have had professional culinary training, she didn't realise how true this was. It later transpired that Dr Roga had no formal medical qualifications at all... he was a pastry chef from Vienna.

One of the weirdest and rarest medical conditions is Foreign Accent Syndrome, whereby sufferers of seizures, strokes or head injuries develop a foreign accent irrespective of any association with the particular country or language concerned. The condition is caused by damage to the part of the brain that controls speech and word formation, and can last for days, weeks or months, or even be permanent. There is no known cure. Between 1941 and 2013 there were sixty-two recorded cases worldwide, including the following:

- Judi Roberts was born in Indiana, USA, but after a stroke in 1999 began to speak in a British accent, even though she'd never been to the UK.

- In 2010 Kay Russell from Gloucestershire took a nap after a migraine attack and, on awakening, spoke with a distinct French accent.

- The same thing happened to Leanne Rowe from Tasmania, who spoke with a French accent after recovering from a head injury following a car accident.

- Some victims acquire multiple accents and one of the most famous is Linda Walker, a sixty-year-old from Newcastle who recovered after a stroke in 2006 to discover her usual Geordie intonation had vanished and been replaced by a series of random accents, including Jamaican, Canadian and Eastern European.

People affected by fatal familial insomnia, or FFI, can never fall asleep, a condition that leads to hallucinations, panic attacks, dementia and, inevitably, death.

In 2012 Oregon resident Paul Gaylord was bitten by a stray cat and contracted a rare case of the medieval bubonic plague, also known as the 'Black Death'. He survived but lost his fingers and toes.

Before radium was seen as a deadly radioactive health hazard, it was put into water to create a drink that was marketed as a fountain of youth which provided an 'indefinable spark of life'.

Eunuchs were a part of the Chinese Imperial Court for thousands of years, right up until the twentieth century. Eunuchs traditionally had their penises pickled in a jar and carried in a bag hung on their belt. This way, when a eunuch died, he could be buried with his genitals and be reincarnated as a 'full man'.

It could be cats, heights or flying, but most people are afraid of something. There's a name for the most common phobias – and a lot of the uncommon ones:

- Arachibutyrophobia: fear of peanut butter sticking to the roof of your mouth

- Aulophobia: fear of flutes

- Automatonophobia: fear of ventriloquist's dummies

- Barophobia: fear of gravity

- Bibliophobia: fear of books

- Chionophobia: a fear of snow

- Consecotaleophobia: fear of chopsticks

- Coulrophobia: fear of clowns

- Ephebiphobia: fear of teenagers

- Ereuthophobia: fear of the colour red

- Genuphobia: fear of knees

- Gnosiophobia: fear of knowledge

- Isopterophobia: fear of termites

- Linonophobia: fear of string

- Macrophobia: fear of long waits

- Metrophobia: fear of poetry

- Peladophobia: fear of bald people

- Pentheraphobia: fear of your mother-in-law

- Phobophobia: fear of fear

- Pogonophobia: fear of beards

- Pteronophobia: fear of (being tickled by) feathers

- Sesquipedaliophobia: fear of long words

At the end of the nineteenth century, X-ray technology was in its infancy and manufacturers were keen to promote this pioneering medical invention to the public. In 1896 a man named Herbert Hawks decided to demonstrate his company's machine by setting it up in a busy shopping precinct and focusing X-rays on his head so the public could see his skull on a screen. Unaware of the effects of being bombarded by the rays, the full impact of the demonstration became apparent to Mr Hawks after just a few days. By then he'd lost his hair, eyebrows and eyelashes, damaged his eyesight, had bleeding gums and his skin was peeling off his chest.

CRIME AND PUNISHMENT

Joshua Jones was sentenced to capital punishment in 1839 and served out his last days in Coudersport Prison, Pennsylvania. Finding out on the day of his execution that he only had one dollar to his name, his last meal was very symbolic. He ate the dollar bill between two slices of bread.

Someone with more of an appetite was Gary Carl Simmons. His last meal in Mississippi State Penitentiary in 2012 consisted of a Pizza Hut medium Super Supreme Deep Dish pizza, double portion, with mushrooms, onions, jalapeño peppers and pepperoni; another pizza, but this time a regular portion, with three cheeses, olives, peppers, tomato, garlic and Italian sausage; one supersize order of McDonald's fries with extra ketchup and mayonnaise; one family-size pack of Doritos, nacho cheese flavour; 8 oz jalapeño nacho cheese dip; 4 oz sliced jalapeños; ten 8-oz packs of Parmesan cheese; ten 8-oz packs of ranch dressing; two pints of strawberry ice cream – and, to wash it down, two large strawberry shakes and two pints of Cherry Coke... a grand total of 29,000 calories.

A Parisian grocer was jailed in 1978 for murder, having allegedly stabbed his wife with a wedge of cheese.

To prevent violence among inmates it was customary during certain phases of the moon for hospital staff to chain and flog inmates of England's infamous Bedlam asylum.

A prisoner who escaped from Utah State Penitentiary surprised guards by calling them from an unspecified location 'just to check how things were'.

The opposite occurred when Jerry Wolfson broke out of Norwich prison. Two hours after his daring escape he was back at the prison gates pleading to be let back in, complaining that he was cold and wet and his escape had left him with an embarrassing rip in his trousers.

When Richard Ramirez, the infamous US mass murderer known as the 'Night Stalker', failed a metal detector test on entry to the San Francisco County Jail, a series of X-rays was needed to identify the reason. These revealed a number of objects in Ramirez's rectum, including a syringe, a handcuff key, a pen and a piece of cellophane on which was written 'I love chocolate'.

In February 1979 six Peruvian gunmen used a light aircraft to rob an isolated farm in the mountainous north of the country. They escaped with the equivalent of £500 then discovered it had cost them considerably more to hire the aircraft and fill it with fuel.

Robbers who took part in a £175,000 raid on a jeweller's near Rainham in Kent in December 2008 hired a getaway driver with a difference... he had no arms. In spite of his disability, the eighteen-year-old driver managed to lead the police on a terrifying 30-mile chase reaching speeds of up to 100 mph, with other gang members changing gear for him. The gang was eventually caught when police forced their car off the road and into a wall. The driver wasn't wearing his prosthetic arms at the time of the getaway and it was never ascertained why the robbers might have considered him to be the best man for the job in the first place.

In the Aztec empire, public drunkenness (unless it happened on the last five days of the year) was punished by having one's head shaved and house destroyed.

In January 1997 a man ran into a shop in Cookstown, County Tyrone, and stole boxer shorts and socks. He was immediately identified by staff because, at 2.26 metres (7 feet 4 inches) tall, he was Ireland's tallest man.

Al Capone's business card said he was a used furniture dealer.

Al Capone – here for all your furniture needs!

Javier Ortiz, aged twenty-five, of Badajoz, Spain, had just robbed a bank and, to avoid capture, he decided to hide in a nearby convent and wait until the coast was clear. All went well initially as Ortiz managed to get in undetected, but it started to go wrong when hunger got the better of him. Stealing a nun's habit, he found the convent's kitchen and coolly walked in and stole a leg of ham. Hearing footsteps, Ortiz decided to hide the ham down his habit, turn his head away and act nonchalantly. The footsteps belonged to the Mother Superior, who was fairly sure she didn't have any pregnant nuns in the convent and called the police.

In Ancient Greece adulterous men were sometimes punished by the removal of their pubic hair and the insertion of a large radish into their rectum.

In Brazil in November 1993, solvent addict Sergio de Sa broke into a glue factory. He tried various samples before eventually finding a vat of his favourite glue being processed – and immediately started inhaling. Overcome by fumes, he passed out and, as he fell to the ground, managed to pull the whole tank over. By the time de Sa regained consciousness he was stuck fast to the factory floor. Staff arriving the next morning found him lying helplessly and called the police, who pried him free – then arrested him.

In November 1985 thieves broke into the White Space Art Gallery in north London but ignored artwork worth hundreds of thousands of pounds on display. Instead, they made off with just a £150 security grill.

The electric chair was invented by a dentist.

In 1985 it was reported that the American NBC network spent $1.5 million on each individual episode of the successful *Miami Vice* crime show. That year Miami's real vice squad had a budget of $1.16 million to fight crime for the entire year.

A firearms shop full of customers is never a good choice for a robbery but, in February 1990, this didn't stop a would-be thief from trying. The man entered the gun shop in Renton, Seattle, and calmly fired a pistol in the air, announcing that a hold-up was in progress. As if a shop full of gun-carrying customers wasn't bad enough, a uniformed King County policeman was also present, chatting to the staff. As soon as he had fired his gun, the assailant was shot dead by the cop and a sales assistant.

Vatican City has a higher crime rate than any other nation of the world.

In the 1930s a celebrated and eloquent Irish barrister defended a man accused of bestiality with a duck. He told the court that the case should be thrown out, as it was clear that a duck was not a beast, but a fowl. The jury agreed and his client was acquitted.

One of the cruellest methods of torture and eventual execution was the Brazen Bull, sometimes known as the Bronze Bull or Sicilian Bull. Designed in Ancient Greece, the metalworker Perillos of Athens cast a hollow bull from solid brass, with a lockable door on one side. At the start of the execution, the victim was placed inside the bull and a fire was lit underneath. This was fed until the metal literally glowed yellow, causing the victim to slowly roast to death. To entertain spectators, the head of the bull was designed with a complex system of tubes so that the prisoner's screams sounded just like a bellowing bull.

Eighty-six-year-old Lawrence Loeffler shot his wife, eighty-three-year-old Betty, for putting the lid on the ketchup bottle too tightly.

In eighteenth-century London, criminals who had been condemned to be hanged were offered a last drink on their way to the gallows at the Church of St Giles-in-the-Field. It was recorded that one prisoner who was teetotal refused this offer and asked his guards to take him straight to the place of execution since he wanted to get the whole deed over as quickly as possible. By not stopping he missed – by just two minutes – the reprieve that had granted a stay of execution.

When serial killer Hamilton Howard 'Albert' Fish was sentenced to the electric chair in Sing Sing Prison, New York, in 1936, the first surge of electricity failed to kill him. It was discovered that twenty-nine pins and needles that Fish had previously inserted into his genitals had caused a short circuit.

A chef in the town of Etah, India, was shot by a customer for not putting onions in his omelette.

An infamous method of execution in China until it was banned in 1905 was 'Death by a Thousand Cuts'. Known as *ling chi*, which translates as 'slow slicing', it involved the executioner being presented with a basket of razor-sharp knives, each inscribed with the name of a body part. Knives were selected at random and the relevant body part was slowly removed. The random nature meant that death could be quick or prolonged, with the victim suffering throughout the ordeal, however long it lasted. Rich relatives would often bribe the executioner to 'find' the knife bearing the word 'heart' as quickly as possible.

After robbing a bank in Cooperville, Texas, the thief ran out into the street and pulled open the door of the first car he saw in the slow-moving traffic. He planned to commandeer it and drive himself to safety, but unfortunately the vehicle he chose was a police car.

The Chico City Council in California has enforced a ban on nuclear weapons, setting a $500 fine for anyone detonating one within the city limits.

LAW AND ORDER

A woman in Mauritius was granted an injunction to prevent her farmer husband from making her pull his plough. The court heard that the man refused to use his cow for this task because he believed the animal was the reincarnation of his late mother.

It is illegal to be a prostitute in Siena, Italy, if your name is Mary.

Humans have had sexual congress with animals throughout history. However, some cultures have introduced specific legislation to deal with the relationships. The Ancient Romans took a pragmatic view, imposing a tax on anyone caught having sex with an animal. In Peru it's specifically illegal for males to copulate with a female alpaca, while in Bangkok any male who has sex with a dog is charged with animal cruelty. In Lebanon it's illegal to have sex with a male animal, although sex with female animals is permitted. And in some Middle Eastern countries, it's a sin and a crime to eat any lamb you've had sex with.

The first person sentenced to be locked in the stocks in Boston, England, was Edward Palmer, the builder of the stocks. His crime was charging too much for building them.

In Sicily it was once customary – and acceptable – to bite the nose off your spouse if he or she was unfaithful.

Andrew Vactor, of Urbana in Ohio, was handed a choice of punishments when he was convicted of playing rap music too loudly on his car stereo in July 2008. He could pay a fine of $150 or a fine of just $35 if he spent twenty hours listening to classical music by Bach, Beethoven and Chopin. That way, Municipal Court Judge Susan Fornof-Lippencott said he would understand what it would be like being forced to listen to music he might not prefer, just as other people had had no choice but to listen to his loud rap music. Vactor opted for the lesser fine but only managed about fifteen minutes – and paid the $150 in full.

Prison inmate Richard Barber of Iola, Kansas, tried to kill himself by secretly hoarding enough dental floss to wrap around his neck and hang himself. He only succeeded in cutting his neck. Barber was serving time for murdering his dentist.

In Colombia the average criminal sentence length is 137 years.

In North Carolina, it is against the law for cats and dogs to fight.

One of the consequences of the Egyptian army's ousting of President Morsi in July 2013 was a wave of pro-military nationalism and a corresponding distrust of foreigners of all descriptions... even birds. That was the reason why an Egyptian fisherman carried out a citizen's arrest on a stork seen near his home in Qena, southern Egypt. Spotting an electronic device attached to the bird's back, the fisherman assumed it was a camera, and that the bird was spying for some malevolent foreign government. Grabbing the bird, the man took it to a nearby police station. A vet later identified the device as an innocent wildlife tracker used by scientists to study birds' migratory trends. The stork was released without charge.

In the town of Paulding in Ohio a police officer has the right to stop a barking dog by biting it.

Sir Peregrine Henniker-Heaton was a high-ranking officer in the British Intelligence Service with important connections in the Middle East. On 5 October 1971 he told his wife he was about to go out for a short walk – and was never seen again. Suspecting foul play from a foreign government, the resulting police search proved fruitless, despite reports of Sir Peregrine being sighted in various places, including New York and Paris. Three years after his disappearance his body was found in a disused room in his own west London house, where it had been the whole time. The cause of death was never ascertained and an open verdict was recorded.

In 1865 William E. Brockway printed counterfeit $100 bills that were so perfect that the US Treasury Department's only recourse to prevent them being distributed was to temporarily withdraw every $100 bill from circulation.

Gloria Sykes was hit by a cable car in San Francisco and successfully sued the city for $50,000, not for cuts and bruises, but for turning her into a nymphomaniac. After the accident she told the court that she'd felt compelled to have sex with a hundred different men.

Peking traffic regulations once banned the use of car headlights after dark in order to prevent cyclists being dazzled.

A witness who was sworn in at a Syracuse, New York courthouse had to retake her oath after a court official realised that, instead of swearing on the Bible, she had in fact used a wholly inappropriate book that was lying on the courthouse table at the time; a Danielle Steel romance.

In France you can legally marry a dead person as long as you were engaged to be married to that person before they died. If you think that's weird, in Paris any man carrying onions must be given right of way in the streets, while in Cannes it's illegal to wear a Jerry Lewis mask.

Lawrence O'Dowd was fined £100 by York magistrates in November 1984 for using threatening and abusive language and behaviour likely to occasion a breach of the peace. His crime was shouting 'miaow' to a police dog.

In June 2005 Oxford student Sam Brown told a mounted police officer that his horse was gay... and was promptly arrested and fined £80 for 'causing harassment, harm or distress'.

Employees at a property development company in New Castle, Pennsylvania, were surprised when they couldn't get into their offices. The 50-foot-long by 20-foot-wide (15 x 6 metres) steel bridge they usually drove over was missing. It was suspected that thieves had worked all through the night with welding gear to cut it into pieces and later sell it as scrap metal.

In the 1980s Colombian drug lord Pablo Escobar was spending $2,500 a month on rubber bands just to hold all his cartel's cash.

When a man walked into a police station in Montpellier, France, to report the loss of his vehicle, officers were prepared for another routine case. What they didn't expect was for the owner to say that his vehicle had originally landed on earth 350 years ago. The man identified himself as King Stephane Xerxes of the planet Draxor and said he was desperate for the gendarmerie to retrieve his missing vehicle so that he could return to his home planet. He gave officers a small piece of metal that he claimed was the ignition key, but this was later identified as the ring pull from a Coca-Cola can.

Pinball was illegal in America from the early 1940s to the mid-1970s, with crime bosses running various illegal pinball-machine rackets.

Police in Radnor, Pennsylvania, successfully tricked a suspect into confessing by pretending they had a sophisticated lie detector. They put a metal colander on his head and connected it with wires to a photocopier.

LOSING MY RELIGION

Some medieval Christians believed that the Virgin Mary became pregnant via her ear.

As a result of complaints from fundamentalists supporting gender segregation, Iran's religious leadership ruled in 1981 that male and female mountaineers must climb separately.

A widely reported story in the 1990s concerned a department store in the shopping district of Ginza, Tokyo, that organised a Christmas window display to appeal to Western visitors. Unfortunately the organisers confused the two most prominent images associated with the festival, Jesus Christ and Santa Claus. The result was a life-size mannequin of Santa on a crucifix.

The word 'Christian' appears only three times in the Bible.

The Yaohnanen tribe on the southern island of Tanna in Vanuatu in the South Pacific worship an unusual deity – Prince Philip, the Duke of Edinburgh. They believe he is a divine being, the pale-skinned son of a mountain spirit. According to ancient tales he travelled over the seas to a distant land, married a powerful lady and would in time return. The villagers, aware of the respect afforded Queen Elizabeth II by colonial officials, came to the conclusion that her husband, Prince Philip, must be the son from their legends.

Testamints, as the name suggests, are mints with Bible verses printed on the wrappers, while He'Brew is marketed as 'The best (and only) Jewish Beer in America'.

Four popes allegedly died during sex: Leo VII, John VII, John XIII and Paul II.

Pastor Michael Davis of the Christian Fellowship Church in Larose, Louisiana, planned to baptise a number of followers at the municipal pool. After giving his sermon he stripped down to his trunks and announced, 'Prepare for rebirth, ye faithful, and follow me.' He then stepped into the pool still holding his microphone – and was immediately electrocuted to death due to a faulty earth.

In Santo Domingo in the Dominican Republic, Patrice Tamao wanted to do something symbolic to highlight the need for world peace and understanding. The ultimate show of commitment, he felt, was to have himself nailed to a wooden cross for a mind-numbing seventy-two hours. His sacrifice and his devotion came to a sudden end when one of the wounds caused an infection to Tamao's foot and he had to go to the hospital for treatment.

In Ancient Egypt beautiful female corpses were not handed to the embalmers right away, but left for three or four days. This was not part of some religious ceremony or symbolism, but merely a precaution to prevent the embalmers, who had a reputation for this sort of thing, from having sex with the bodies before they prepared them for their journey to the afterlife.

> By placing the beds of dying patients on scales and noting their weights immediately before and after death, the Swedish physician Nils-Olof Jacobson concluded that the human soul weighs just 21 g (0.74 oz).

In England during the 1700s you could insure yourself against going to hell.

Ancient Egyptians were forbidden to eat pike or bream because, according to legend, when the god Osiris was thrown into the Nile these were the fish that had eaten his penis.

Confession is a smartphone app that has the blessing of the Catholic Church. It allows sinners to examine their conscience and keep track of their sins.

The Aetherius Society is a UFO religion founded in 1954 that combines alien wisdom with yoga.

In 1997 Leonso Canales Jr of Kingsville, Texas, succeeded in replacing the traditional greeting of hello with something less evil. Fifty-six-year-old Mr Canales said, 'When you go to school and church, they tell you "hell" is negative and "heaven" is positive. I think it's time that we set a new precedent, to tell our kids that we are positive adults.' The Kleberg County commissioners agreed and unanimously designated 'heaven-o' as the county's official greeting.

One of the patron saints of Sicily is St Agatha. During the third century, Agatha chose to defend her virginity by opposing a high-ranking Roman. As a result, she was sent to prison, where her breasts were removed – but were later restored by divine intervention. Every year, Sicilians honour her memory on a feast day, by carrying images of her breasts through the streets.

St Apollonia, who died in AD 249, lived in Alexandria, Egypt, and refused to renounce her Christianity. She was punished by having all her teeth violently pulled out one by one. She is now the patron saint of dentists.

Showman Jules Warner presented his clairvoyant horse Henny at fairgrounds and carnivals, inviting visitors to think of a number from one to ten. Henny would successfully guess the number by tapping it out with her hoof. At one show in 1881 in the town of Athens, Tennessee, a rumour spread that Henny was possessed by the Devil and soon the horse was blamed for all sorts of the townspeople's woes. An angry mob stoned the horse and killed it. Locals then insisted that the horse's body was burned to purge it of the Devil.

The Spanish Inquisition saved some of their most inventive torture techniques for a Christian sect called the Waldensians, which originated in Lyon, France, in the late twelfth century. One of their methods of persuading victims to convert to Catholicism was lighting small bags of gunpowder placed in their mouths. Another was drilling holes in their heels and dragging them through the streets by rope. One woman was recorded as being hung head first from a bridge so that soldiers could use her as target practice.

The Canaanites were one of several ancient eastern Mediterranean cultures that worshipped and made religious offerings to piles of animal dung to ensure they would be able to evacuate their bowels on a regular basis.

SUDDENLY I'M NOT HUNGRY ANY MORE

The Downton Hotel in Dawson City, in the Yukon Territory of Canada, is the home of a bar that offers the Sourtoe Cocktail. This consists of just two ingredients; a spirit of your choice and an amputated human toe. Drinkers must abide by the following rule: 'You can drink it fast, you can drink it slow, but the lips have got to touch the toe.' The toes are dehydrated and preserved in alcohol; several have been used and have been replaced when they've been lost – or swallowed. The most recent came from a donor who had learned a handy life lesson: 'Don't wear open-toed sandals when mowing the lawn.'

A 12-oz can of Coca-Cola Classic contains 39 g of high fructose corn syrup, or the equivalent of nine teaspoons of sugar.

Banquets in the imperial court of the Chinese emperor Shi Hu (reigned AD 295–349) were memorable. The emperor would select a girl from his harem, have her beheaded and then cook and serve her torso. Shi Hu would then display the head on a platter for all the guests to see, to prove he had sacrificed one of his prettiest mistresses.

Eskimo mothers sometimes use their own mouths to suck the mucus out of their babies' noses.

A cobra's heart is a popular Vietnamese delicacy. It's usually eaten while still beating, accompanied by a glass of cobra blood or cooked with some rice wine.

Some tapeworms can reach a length of 40 feet (12 metres) – 10 feet (3 metres) longer than the average human intestine.

In 1981 James Bedlow of Stevenage attempted to eat 14 lbs (6.4 kg) of donated earwax. He got within a whisker of 13 lbs (5.9 kg) when he vomited and was unable to continue.

Although the practice ceased there in the nineteenth century, Fijian cannibals used a wooden fork when devouring people as a mark of respect for the dead. Ordinarily, they would just have eaten with their hands.

Toothpaste in Roman times was made from human urine (usually mixed with crushed bones or oyster shells), and was used as a mouthwash in its liquid form (the ammonia within urine is a powerful cleanser). The urine from the Portuguese was considered the strongest and therefore the most expensive. Urine as an ingredient in toothpaste continued to be used throughout the eighteenth century.

Carmine, a bright-red food colourant, is actually the crushed abdomen of the female cochineal *(Dactylopius coccus)*, a South American beetle-like insect.

Any product labelled 'processed cheese' only has to contain 51 per cent cheese. The rest consists of additives, flavouring, emulsifiers, colouring and extra salt.

During an average lifespan we defecate about 360 lbs (163 kg) of faeces and pass about 132 gallons (600 litres) of urine.

The Cocoma tribe of Peru used to drink the ground-up bones of dead relatives on the basis that it was better for the deceased to end up inside a warm friend than the cold ground.

During a siege by Henry of Navarre in 1596, it's believed that starving Parisians fed themselves by making bread from ground-down bones taken from the crypt of the Holy Innocents' Cemetery.

The Masai tribesmen of East Africa enjoy a mixture of cattle blood and sweet milk as a staple of their diet.

As a mark of reverence, the Uape Indians of the Upper Amazon mix a locally brewed alcoholic beverage called casiri with the ashes of their deceased.

Elizabethan women used to drink puppy urine in the belief that it would improve their complexions.

When US fast-food chain Hardee's introduced its Monster Thickburger in 2004, it was described as a 'monument to decadence'. Consisting of two 1/3-lb (150 g) slabs of Angus beef, three slices of cheese, four strips of bacon, mayonnaise and butter, the burger delivers 1,420 calories and 3.8 oz (107 g) of fat. If you add a portion of fries, you'll be consuming 4.8 oz (135 g) of fat – more than twice the recommended daily intake. A spokesman for the Center for Science in the Public Interest commented: 'If the old Thickburger was "food porn", the new Monster Thickburger is the fast-food equivalent of a snuff movie.'

Azodicarbonamide, a flour-bleaching chemical found in fast-food buns, is also present in yoga mats and the soles of trainers.

After Lord Nelson died at the Battle of Trafalgar his body was placed in a barrel of rum in order to preserve it on its way back to England. This didn't dissuade the thirsty crew from drinking from the barrel on the long journey home. Today 'Nelson's Blood' is the name given to a cocktail of rum and spices (there are various recipes) traditionally drunk on 21 October in celebration of the battle.

In April 2011 a Force 3 tornado ripped through Jackson, Mississippi. Eric Hubbard was one of its many victims but it wasn't the fact that the violent storm took out the back of his house, put a tree through his living room or destroyed his car that made him angry... it was the fact that the tornado ripped a hamburger and fries right out of his hands.

How to stop a polite dinner party dead in its tracks: when asked what you do, tell guests you're a turkey-milker. Explain that this role involves collecting sperm to inseminate female turkeys by stimulating male turkeys to ejaculation. (N.B. the job pays about £9 an hour.)

There was an ancient Chinese dish called 'Three Screams' ('san zhi er') in which newborn mice were served alive. The dish was given its name to reflect the three times the mouse screamed out:

/ The first scream came when the helpless animal was picked up between chopsticks.

/ The second scream came when it was dipped in a chilli sauce.

/ The third (and last) scream came when it entered the diner's mouth.

The Roman emperor Vitellius and Anne Boleyn had a strange thing in common – they used to vomit in between courses to make room for more food. Vitellius would do this by sticking a long feather down his throat, while Anne Boleyn could apparently do it at will.

Kopi Luwak is an Asian beverage brewed from partially digested coffee beans that have been excreted by the Asian palm civet (a member of the cat family). Fans of the drink claim that the cat's stomach acids impart a special flavour and distinct aroma to the beans that cannot be matched.

Many fast-food restaurants add the chemical propylene glycol to their salads in order to maintain moisture. The same chemical is used as a sexual lubricant and in antifreeze.

In 1998 Channel 4 was severely reprimanded for an episode of *TV Dinners* in which a woman's afterbirth was served up as pâté. The presenter, Hugh Fearnley-Whittingstall, devised the recipe with mother Rosie Clear for a party to celebrate the birth of her daughter. It consisted of frying the placenta with shallots and garlic, following which the dish was flambéed, puréed and served to twenty relatives and friends as a pâté on focaccia bread. Mrs Clear's husband Lee had seventeen helpings but the other guests were less enthusiastic.

In parts of Asia, raw ape brain is still regarded as a delicacy and aphrodisiac. The ape is killed immediately prior to the meal in order for its brain to be served fresh.

In parts of the Philippines rat-meat sausages are considered a delicacy.

China produces a deer-penis wine, which purportedly is part aphrodisiac, part energy drink and part effective remedy for athletic injuries.

ASTONISHING ANATOMIES

Adam Rainer was born in Graz, Austria-Hungary, in 1899 to normal-sized parents and tried to join the army in 1917, aged eighteen. He was rejected due to his height – he was just over 4 feet (1.2 metres), being classified as a dwarf. However, a sudden growth spurt when he was twenty-one resulted in him reaching 7 feet 2 inches (2.2 metres) by the time he was thirty-two. A tumour on his pituitary gland was thought responsible for this remarkable change in height; when he died, aged fifty-two, he was 7 feet 8 inches (2.3 metres) – making him the only man to have been officially classified as both a dwarf and a giant.

Dead human bodies don't deteriorate as quickly as they used to, due to the fact that our modern diet contains so many preservatives.

Giuseppe de Mai of Naples was born with a healthy heart... and another just like it. In 1894 he signed a contract with the London Academy of Medicine and was paid $15,000 for his permission for them to study his two hearts after his death.

In 2002 Ma Zhong Nan, an eighty-nine-year-old man living in a small Chinese village, accidentally cut his scalp while combing his hair and discovered a hard substance flowing from the small wound. Six months later it had formed into a 4-inch-long (10-cm-long) horn sprouting from the top of his head.

A similar case involved a sixty-nine-year-old woman who visited her doctor in 2008 with an 8-inch (20-cm) horn growing out from the centre of her forehead. Like Nan, she thought this had been the result of a head injury twenty years previously. The horn was successfully surgically removed.

Louise L (her real identity was never known) was recognised in nineteenth-century France as 'La Dame à Quatre Jambes' – the four-legged woman. Born in 1869, Louise had two extra atrophied limbs hanging down between her own legs. Louise earned a considerable amount of money on the circus circuit and eventually gave birth to two perfectly formed daughters.

Paediatric brain surgeon Dr Paul Grabb of the Memorial Hospital for Children in Colorado Springs, Colorado, removed a small foot he found growing inside the brain of a three-day-old baby.

French cabaret artist Le Pétomane (1857–1945) had a very unusual act; he would break wind to music and thereby became one of the highest-paid artists in Paris. Born Joseph Pujol, having both the ability to draw air straight into his rectum and a remarkable control of his sphincter muscles, Le Pétomane (which translates as 'fartomaniac') could fart at will and managed to hold a single note for sixteen seconds. He could also mimic the sounds of animals and musical instruments, play 'La Marseillaise', and extinguish a candle from several yards. In his twenty-seven-year career Le Pétomane performed in front of some illustrious spectators, including Edward, Prince of Wales, King Leopold II of Belgium and Sigmund Freud.

The largest boil on medical records belonged to a Mr Rodney Howells of Bristol. It was 3.5 inches (8.9 cm) in diameter and, when lanced by Dr Arthur Reynolds in June 1924, yielded 'almost a pint of pungent pus'.

Wang Fang of Chongqing, China, was born with her feet facing backwards. Although officially classified as disabled, she refused to accept a disability pension, saying, 'I can walk as well as anyone else, and even run faster than them. I'm like everyone else – except of course that I put my shoes on backwards.'

In 2003 Maria Alaimo of Staten Island, New York, visited a plastic surgeon for a breast-augmentation operation, but came out with more than she bargained for… twice as many breasts. Mrs Alaimo wanted full 36C cups but ended up with what were essentially four breasts. She sued the surgeon for $5 million for 'pain, disability, loss of self-esteem, humiliation and embarrassment,' and in 2010 she was awarded $3.5 million in damages.

Forty-two-year-old Barbie Edwards of Washington has forty thousand online fans… or rather her bottom does. Claiming to have the world's largest bottom, she says her fuller figure has its uses. 'I often use my butt shelf to balance food on while I'm preparing family meals. It's also great for balancing cleaning products on when I'm tidying the house or snacks when I'm lying on the sofa at night.' But Barbie's bottom doesn't just have practical uses. It's also a real money-earner. Her fans pay for photos and to see her balance things on her butt like plates of doughnuts or pizzas. She commented, 'At first I found these requests strange, but now I love it because I know it's making my fans happy.'

Jack Ellis of Columbia, Tennessee, lived up to his nickname of 'The Human Cannon'; he could place a suitably lubricated 4.75-inch (12-cm) 'cannonball' into his rectum so that it was completely hidden from view – then expel it with such force that it once travelled almost 6 feet (1.8 metres). Dr Frank Morgan of Atlanta, Georgia, took a medical interest in Jack and explained that this feat was possible due to his ability to relax and then contract his anal muscles to an extraordinary degree. Ellis died in 1978, aged just forty-four, after a heart attack thought to have been brought on by his special skill.

Dead people can still get goosebumps. Just as rigor mortis causes muscles to stiffen for a while, the same thing happens to hair follicles. As they contract, the skin around them takes on the appearance of goosebumps.

The blood contained in a human erection is enough to keep three gerbils alive.

Emilion Guastucci from Lucca, Italy, astounded doctors when he was born — every organ was on the opposite side of his body. His heart and spleen were on the right; his appendix and liver were on the left. Despite that he lived a perfectly normal and healthy life.

Because many Japanese sumo wrestlers (average weight about 325 lbs/147 kg) are too fat to wipe their backsides, the duty (and some say, honour) goes to novice wrestlers. According to reports, six out of ten novices decide to leave their apprenticeship...

Conjoined twins can take two forms; where both twins are alive and functioning, and where one twin is just a parasitic appendage that juts out from somewhere on the host's body. Some of the most famous have included:

- Betty Lou Williams: born in 1932 in Georgia, USA, her twin, consisting of just buttocks and legs, grew out of her waist.

- Edward Mordrake: he had a second face on the back of his head that could laugh and cry, but which couldn't eat or speak – although Mordrake claimed it whispered Satanic language to him at night. He committed suicide aged twenty-three.

- Macha and Dacha: these Russian sisters had two complete upper bodies but shared one set of legs.

- Pasquel Piñon: born in Mexico in 1889 with an extra head on top of his forehead – although many believe this was a fake added by an exploitative circus promoter.

- Myrtle Corbin: from Texas, she had a twin growing out from between her legs, giving her four legs and two vaginas. She was said to be able to move the two smaller inner legs but they were too weak for walking. She married in 1882 and gave birth to five children, three from one body and two from the other.

❗ Laloo: Born in India in 1874, he had a functioning small headless twin attached to his chest, with two arms and two legs.

Known as 'the girl who cries blood', Twinkle Dwivedi from Lucknow, India, bleeds up to fourteen times a day from her eyes, hairline, nose, neck and soles of her feet without a single cut and without feeling any pain. This mysterious bleeding started when she was eleven and, despite a multitude of tests, MRI and ultrasound scans, none of the specialists who have examined her are any the wiser in determining the cause – or the cure.

ODDITIES OF THE RICH AND FAMOUS

Unbeknown to Frank O'Neill, the former Australian Olympic swimming champion, his independently wealthy wife Patricia O'Neill (daughter of the Countess of Kenmore) decided to leave her £40 million fortune to her pet chimp, Kalu. The ape, however, sadly won't benefit as much as her owner thought she might... in 2010 eighty-five-year-old Mrs O'Neill discovered that most of her immense fortune had gone missing over the years, having been taken 'by crooked advisors' in small amounts over a long period of time. She said, 'I'm a woman who does not really know about money. I'm not good with dates and figures.' Until this revelation, Kalu, twenty-five, was widely thought to be the second-richest pet in the world.

When Catherine the Great discovered she was suffering from dandruff, she had her royal hairdresser locked in an iron cage to prevent him from telling anyone about it.

In 1979 the father of actor Woody Harrelson confessed to police that he had assassinated President Kennedy.

Apart from owning over three thousand pairs of shoes and almost a thousand handbags, Imelda Marcos of the Philippines also had a collection of bulletproof bras. After she fled into exile in 1986, her collections were stored in the presidential palace and in Manila's National Museum. However, a combination of inadequate protection and flooding from tropical storms has meant that most of the shoes have been destroyed by water, humidity, mould or termites.

In order to enhance the Führer's virility, Hitler's personal physician, Theodor Morell, gave him regular injections of excrement and extracts of crushed human genitalia. He is also known to have prescribed pills containing cocaine, as wells as copious quantities of anti-flatulence medication.

Actor Mark Wahlberg has three nipples. The third very small nipple (known as a nubbin) is below his left nipple and had to be photoshopped out of his famous Calvin Klein ads. Other celebrities admitting to having 50 per cent more nipples are actress Tilda Swinton, actor Bill Paxton, and singers Lily Allen and Harry Styles (who has two extra but they're tiny.)

In order to conceal just how fat he'd become, it was reported that Marlon Brando insisted on only being filmed above the waist when he appeared in the 2001 film, *The Score*. To make sure his requests were followed, he would appear on set without any trousers.

Jim Carrey is known to keep a chef on the set of his movies – to prepare special dishes for his dog. On the set of *Ace Ventura: When Nature Calls*, he reportedly retained the services of a chef for his pet iguana.

To try to overcome depression, Janet Jackson (sister of Michael) had a coffee enema. She told a reporter, 'Your body cells hold emotions and with the enema you can bring out the sad cells – or whatever it is.' While not usually associated with treating depression, coffee enemas are a proven strong antioxidant. However, a word of warning... their overuse can result in the body absorbing a lethal dose of caffeine.

According to Paul Johnson, in his book *Intellectuals*, millionaire publisher Victor Gollancz had a phobia that his penis would disappear one day. He apparently took it out several times a day just to make sure it was still there...

During World War Two, comic actor W. C. Fields kept $50,000 in German banks, 'just in case the little bastard wins.'

Jerry Lewis couldn't think what to send a very wealthy friend for his birthday, so he hired a homeless, alcoholic dwarf and packed him in a crate with a note: 'For the man who has everything.'

Madonna told David Letterman on his show in 1994 that she urinates on her feet to cure athlete's foot.

Eccentric French millionaire Henri Blanchard liked to boast he had nerves of steel. To prove it, on 9 May 1903, he climbed alone into a circus cage with eight lions and fired a pistol at a target, hitting dead centre each time.

The eccentric British eighteenth-century geologist William Buckland would dine on a wide variety of species including roast crocodile, bear, hedgehog, panther, porpoise and even puppies. He bragged that he would eat anything that moved except two things: moles and bluebottles.

American novelist Mark Twain was the first known author to submit a typed manuscript.

The Greek philosopher Diogenes, one of the founders of Cynicism, rejected material comforts. He slept in a large ceramic jar and destroyed the only wooden bowl he possessed after seeing how a peasant boy drank from just his cupped hands. Diogenes admired the simple honesty of dogs and imitated them, thinking nothing about squatting down and going to the toilet in a busy marketplace.

Anne Boleyn had eleven fingers.

Charlie and the Chocolate Factory author Roald Dahl also wrote the screenplay adaptation for the 1967 James Bond film *You Only Live Twice*.

Theodor Geisel, aka Dr Seuss, would try to cure writer's block by sitting in his closet wearing a variety of strange hats.

Aristotle Onassis had a novel chat-up line. After buying ex-King Farouk's frigate, he had it completely refitted, covering bar stools with the foreskin of a white whale. On one occasion he turned to Greta Garbo and told her that she was now sitting on the largest penis in the world.

Idi Amin (1925–2003), president and psychopathic dictator of Uganda, had the self-bestowed grand title of 'His Excellency, President for Life, Field Marshal Al Hadji Doctor Idi Amin Dada, VC, DSO, MC, Lord of All the Beasts of the Earth and Fishes of the Seas and Conqueror of the British Empire in Africa in General and Uganda in Particular'.

It was reported that Johnny Depp is descended from the first female slave in the United States to sue for her freedom and win.

Benjamin Disraeli had the legs of his bed placed in bowls full of salty water to ward off evil spirits.

Elvis Presley owned a pet chimpanzee called Scatter. The 40-lb (18-kg) chimp would get drunk and bite members of his entourage. He wore tailor-made suits and would sometimes sit on the lap of Elvis's driver wearing a small chauffeur's cap. The driver would sometimes duck down when another car pulled alongside so it looked like Scatter was steering.

The tyrannical, cruel and perverse third Roman emperor Caligula (AD 12–41) made his horse Incitatus a consul and a priest.

Dictator Kim Il Sung had every road in North Korea built with a separate lane just for his exclusive use.

The poet Virgil (70–19 BC) held a lavish funeral for his pet housefly that cost the equivalent of £65,000. Attended by the great and the good of Rome, moving eulogies were given for the dead fly, which was buried in an elaborate tomb which boasted this inscription: 'Fly, may this urn prove light for you, and may your bones rest easily.'

Salvador Dalí sometimes wore home-made cologne of fish glue and goat manure in order to attract his then girlfriend (later his wife) Gala. He said he wanted to recreate the smell of a ram that walked past his house every morning.

The mental stability of Libya's Colonel Gaddafi was always in question – by his allies as well as his enemies. President Anwar Sadat of Egypt tried to get his friend to have a brain scan but the CIA was in absolutely no doubt as to his state of mind. A 1985 report discloses that he made a secret trip to Majorca wearing make-up and carrying a teddy bear.

For some souvenir hunters a simple autograph or signed photo just won't do. When Albert Einstein died, his brain was removed for study by the pathologist on duty, Thomas Harvey. However, it soon went missing and was later found in Harvey's apartment, kept in a jar inside an old cider box hidden under a beer cooler. Harvey also removed Einstein's eyeballs and gave them to his ophthalmologist, who kept them in his dresser drawer for decades.

The richest pet in the world is thought to be a German shepherd dog called Gunther IV, believed to be worth around £90 million, deriving from the fortune of a German countess.

SEX AND SENSIBILITY

Edward Smith from Washington State has a very unusual girlfriend; it's his 1969 Volkswagen Beetle named Vanilla. A true 'mechaphile', he claims that he first had sex with a car when he was fifteen and has never been attracted to women or men. He doesn't stop at cars, though, claiming that his most intense sexual experience was 'making love' to the helicopter from hit 1980s TV show *Airwolf*.

The average speed of a human ejaculation is 28 mph.

A young Japanese couple, Sachi and Tomio Hidaka, got married in 1978 but both were so shy that it took fourteen years before they consummated their marriage, at the age of thirty-four. Sadly, the excitement of having sex for the first time proved too great and they both reportedly died from heart attacks brought on by shock.

In a lifetime we spend an average of two weeks kissing.

Orlando's Channel 6 in Florida reported that sexually transmitted diseases were running rampant among seniors at The Villages, a 60,000-strong retirement community known as a conservative Republican enclave. A gynaecologist interviewed by the station confirmed that she treats more cases of herpes in the retirement community than she did when practising in Miami. The three reasons given were Viagra, a lack of sex education, and no risk of pregnancy.

Cucumbers, carrots and bananas – and even vibrators, bottles and candles – are positively pedestrian compared to some of the things that have been officially reported as having been surgically removed from embarrassed patients' rectums. Objects have included:

- French bread

- Frozen pig's tail

- Soldering iron

- Tin of condensed milk

- Impulse Body Spray bottle

- Artillery shell

- Half-full tobacco pouch

- Sand-filled bicycle inner tube

- Teacup

- Jar of peanut butter (crunchy variety)

- Light bulb

- Pair of spectacles

- Seventy-two fine jewellers saws (all from the same patient)

- Torch

- Mobile phone

- Pistol

- Live eel

- Cassette tape

- Sunglasses

- Barbie doll

- Buzz Lightyear toy

One of the oddest cases of foreign bodies found in rectums involved a concrete enema. A man poured a mixture of cement and sand into his friend's rectum via a funnel but for a reason only known to the two of them, the mixture was left to harden into concrete. After it was removed during a difficult operation, the enema victim was left with a unique and very personal souvenir of their exploits; a perfect concrete cast of his rectum.

Celery makes a man more attractive to a woman; chewing it sets off a chemical reaction that stimulates pheromones that women find desirable.

The Kellogg Company promotes the health benefits of its breakfast cereals by talking about the nutritional advantages of grains and fibres, minerals and vitamins... but it wasn't always like this. John Harvey Kellogg was a fervent crusader against the perils of masturbation and started manufacturing cornflakes in 1897 in order to provide a meat-free breakfast that he believed would reduce the prevalence of this heinous act.

When men of Central Australia's Walibri tribe greet each other, they shake each other's penises instead of hands.

It seems there's no such thing as 'too much fun' in the bedroom. Flavoured and even luminous condoms look positively staid when you're able to buy condoms shaped like dinosaurs, bananas, monkeys or the Devil – or, especially for Easter, condoms shaped like a hen or ribbed to resemble a crown of thorns. For those wanting to impress, you can buy condoms printed with a ruler (presumably one that takes stretching into account), and for the stylish, there are condoms printed to resemble a tuxedo or a Louis Vuitton bag. For those for whom ego is everything, you can even have condoms printed with your face and name.

It has been widely reported that on his wedding night in 1848 the Victorian author and art critic John Ruskin found the sight of his wife Effie's pubic hair so shocking that he vowed never to sleep with her again. The marriage was annulled after six years due to non-consummation. One reason suggested for Ruskin's reaction is that he had previously only known the female form through Greek statues and nude paintings, which always omitted pubic hair.

Paleolithic art dating back thirty thousand years shows that man invented sex toys long before the wheel.

It's amazing what lengths people will go to in order to get turned on. The following have all been promoted as aphrodisiacs:

- Whale excrement

- Toad excrement

- A sheep's eyelid soaked in hot tea

- Pigeon excrement

- Live monkey brains

- Lizards soaked in urine

- Bull penis and testicle soup

- Cobra meat

- Menstrual blood

- Dolphin testicles

- Pigeon dung

/ Melted fat from a camel hump

/ Dried tiger's penis

/ Ambergris (intestinal secretions of the sperm whale)

The Tre-ba society in Tibet only allows one marriage per family. That means if you have brothers, you all have to marry the same wife.

The Dahari tribe in India have a similar practice. All the brothers in a family pool their resources to buy a wife, who they then share.

There are several odd laws still on the US statute books that pertain to sex. For example, in Willowdale, Oregon, it's against the law for a husband to talk dirty in his wife's ear during sex; in Tremonton, Utah, it's illegal to have sex in an ambulance; while in Newcastle, Wyoming, you're not permitted to have sex in a butcher shop's meat freezer.

In Ancient Egypt, crocodile dung was used as a contraceptive, while in Ancient Rome, goats' bladders were favoured for this purpose.

One of the most public examples of bestiality took place in Valencia, Spain, when Paulo 'Chico' Lopez had sexual intercourse with a bull in the middle of the city's main bullring in front of 20,000 cheering spectators. It was reported that he managed to achieve success 'after several unsuccessful attempts and some nasty kicks'.

One in ten European babies are conceived in an IKEA bed.

The largest dildo currently on sale is the 'Great American Challenge'. It's almost 16 inches (41 cm) long (if you're interested, that's 11.5 insertable inches/29 insertable centimetres), with a diameter of 3 inches (7.6 cm) and a circumference of 9 inches (23 cm). It's purple, if you feel the need to go shopping for one.

Some people chase thrills regardless of the consequences and such a case was reported in the *Japan Times* in April 1997. The story concerned a Thai boy, who was heavily into the craze known as  'pumping'. This involves participants inserting a bicycle pump into their rectums so that the sudden rush of air creates a momentary high. In order to maximise his pleasure, the boy went a step too far. He and some friends went to a petrol station where he inserted a compressed-air line as far as he could. Within moments of him placing a coin into the slot to start the air, he exploded. The police commented, 'When that quantity of air interacted with the gas in his system, it was like an atom bomb went off. We still haven't located all of him.' Don't try this at home (or at your local garage).

THAT'S ENTERTAINMENT!

Mexican entertainer Ramón Barrero's gimmick was that he played the world's smallest harmonica. Well, he did until a performance in 1994 when he accidentally swallowed it and choked to death.

One of the biggest problems with recording the Beatles' *Sgt Pepper's Lonely Hearts Club Band* didn't involve musical differences, just toilet paper. George Harrison was annoyed with the studio's rough, scratchy variety and, after hurried meetings in the EMI boardroom, an executive decision was made to replace the paper with a softer make.

While being held in Spandau Prison in West Berlin, Rudolf Hess, Adolf Hitler's former deputy, was said to be big fan of the US television soap opera *Dynasty*.

Mel Blanc, who voiced Bugs Bunny, was allergic to carrots.

Freddie Mercury and Michael Jackson planned to record a duet for the *Thriller* album, but Mercury decided to pull out when Jackson brought his pet llama to the studio.

Animation producers William Hanna and Joseph Barbera once offered a young Jack Nicholson a job as an animation artist.

John Cleese came very close to being John Cheese. His father changed the family surname because he found it embarrassing.

In 1966 Walt Disney lay on his deathbed, suffering from lung cancer. He asked for a paper and scribbled what would be his last two written words: 'Kurt Russell'. No one knows the significance, let alone Russell, who, in a 2007 appearance on *Jimmy Kimmel Live*, said, 'It's true. I don't know what to make of that. I was taken into his office one time after he died and I was shown that.'

MGM once plotted the menstrual cycles of all its actresses so the studio could plan movies around them.

Mass murderer Charles Manson unsuccessfully auditioned for The Monkees, and one of his songs, 'Never Learn Not To Love', appeared on the Beach Boys 1969 album *20/20*.

When *The Sound of Music* was released in South Korea, it turned out to be too long for local audiences' tastes so the local distributor decided to cut all the songs.

When Cliff Richard discovered his 1975 hit 'Honky Tonk Angel' was actually about prostitutes, he had his own record label withdraw the single... the only known instance of an artist banning his own record.

The Eagles' 1979 album *The Long Run* took so long to record that it became well known in the music business as 'The Long One'. To help speed up the recording process one record company executive even sent them a rhyming dictionary.

REM considered calling themselves 'Cans of Piss' before deciding on their final band name. Many other bands went by equally bizarre names before changing them to something far more catchy and media-friendly:

- Red Hot Chili Peppers – formerly known as Tony Flow and the Miraculously Majestic Masters of Mayhem

- Grateful Dead – formerly known as Mother McCree's Uptown Jug Champions

- Van Halen – formerly known as Rat Salad

- Bee Gees – formerly known as Rattlesnakes

- Nirvana – formerly known as Pen Cap Chew

- Black Sabbath – formerly known as The Polka Tulk Blues Band

- Simple Minds – formerly known as Johnny & The Self-Abusers

Some bands, however, soldier on with bizarre names. Even Crash Test Dummies, The Smashing Pumpkins and The The sound perfectly normal compared to the following pop and rock artists:

⚡ My Dog Has Hitler's Brain

⚡ Flaming Box of Ants

⚡ Brad Pitt Live and Nude

⚡ Hey Look Lettuce!

⚡ Mary Tyler Morphine

⚡ Congratulations on Your Decision to Become a Pilot

⚡ Army of Prawns

⚡ Don't Call Me Francis

⚡ Sorry About Your Daughter

⚡ The Kids Who Never Learned to Color Inside the Lines

⚡ Once I Killed a Gopher With a Stick

⚡ Rainbow Butt Monkeys

⚡ The Makers of the Dead Travel Fast

⚡ The Dead Bodyguards of Abraham Lincoln

- Dead German Tourist

- Fresh Water For the Horses and A Round of Buttermilk For the Men

- Cultivated Bimbo

- Dog Faced Hermans

- God Hates Computers

- Damn You Peter Pan

Errol Flynn is reported to have entertained guests at a Hollywood party by playing the melody of 'You Are My Sunshine' on the piano just with his penis.

The Crusades was a 1935 movie directed by Cecil B. DeMille. In one scene Richard the Lionheart pulls back his cloak to check his watch.

Most fans of the US sitcom *Friends* will know the seventh member of the cast was Ross's pet capuchin monkey,

Marcel. What they probably don't know was that part of Marcel's diet was live worms and if he didn't chew his food properly he was prone to vomiting the worms up on set. After pressure from the human cast members, Marcel was written out after one season.

One of Elvis's favourite pastimes was visiting the Memphis morgue to look at corpses.

Opera fan Armando Botelli's glass eye was shattered when a soprano hit a high note during a performance in Milan.

After Howard Hughes bought the Las Vegas television station KLAS (Channel 8) he insisted they change the programming so it showed films all through the night to cater for his insomnia. If he fell asleep and missed a key part of the film he would just call up the station and order them to rewind the film to the spot where he nodded off.

James Earl Jones, one of the most iconic voices in the movies and the voice of Darth Vader, had a childhood stutter and hardly spoke for eight years.

TV mogul Simon Cowell worked as a runner on *The Shining* and one of his tasks was to polish Jack Nicholson's axe.

In May 1870 the James Robinson & Co Travelling Circus decided to make a real entrance as they arrived in the town of Middletown, Missouri. Despite warnings that the roof wouldn't take the weight, the owner had the circus band perform on top of the lion cage. As predicted, during the performance the cage roof gave way and the circus band found themselves surrounded by several surprised, angry and hungry lions. Out of the ten band members, three were killed there and then and four were fatally mutilated.

On Good Friday in 1930, the BBC reported, 'There is no news.' Instead, they just played piano music.

The lowest-grossing film in history is believed to be the 2006 American indie film *Zyzzyx Road* from director John Penney. A thriller with a reasonable cast including Tom Sizemore and Katherine Heigl, the film took twenty days to film and grossed $30 at the box office from just six patrons – although $10 was refunded to the film's make-up artist, who had paid for herself and a friend to see it.

Polish filmmaker Zbigniew Rybczyński was overjoyed after winning the Oscar for Best Animated Short Film for *Tango* in 1982. After collecting his award Rybczyński stepped outside for a cigarette but was unable to return to the awards ceremony after a security guard interpreted his thick accent as slurred speech and assumed he was a drunk – and refused to let him back in. Rybczynski reportedly yelled, 'American Pig! I have Oscar!' and tried to kick the guard in the groin. He missed the rest of the Oscars after spending the night in jail.

THAT'S GOT
TO HURT!

An American tourist on vacation in South America was admiring the mighty Amazon river when he was stung within an inch of his life by a swarm of killer bees. Seeking safety, he plunged into the water – and was severely bitten by a school of piranhas.

Vlad the Impaler, the fifteenth-century Wallachian prince and inspiration for the Dracula legend, was offended when two Italian ambassadors didn't remove their hats in his presence. Their punishment for this rude behaviour was having their hats nailed to their heads.

In Ancient Syria novice priests who worshipped the goddess Cybele would prove their commitment on the holy Day of Blood. They would ceremonially castrate themselves with a sword (removing the penis along with the testicles) and then run through the streets until they became exhausted. At this point they would throw their severed bits through the window or doorway of the nearest house, much to the surprise (it would be right to assume) of the occupants.

Dr Messenger Monsey, Resident Physician at the Chelsea Royal Hospital in the mid to late 1700s had a rather unconventional approach to tooth extraction. He would take a piece of fishing line, wind one end around the patient's tooth and thread the other end through a hole drilled through a specially prepared bullet. The bullet was then loaded into his revolver and fired.

The bullet ant found in Brazil is so called because its powerful sting has been compared to the overwhelming pain of a gunshot wound.

A woman was admitted to China's Changsha Central Hospital suffering from an itchy ear. A camera inserted into the ear canal revealed a spider had made its home there. To make matters worse, doctors believed the arachnid had been there for a few days.

In 1976 a twenty-two-year-old man was knocked down four times in the space of two minutes. Crossing the busy

Falls Road in Belfast he was hit by a taxi and flung over its roof. As he got up, stunned, he was hit by another car that knocked him into the gutter. As a crowd gathered to see if he was all right a delivery van hit him, followed by another vehicle a moment later. He later made a full recovery from his injuries.

After his victory in the successful siege of Baghdad in 1258, Hulagu Khan, the grandson of Genghis Khan, captured the defeated Caliph Al-Musta'sim but didn't want to spill his royal blood on the ground as he believed the Earth would be offended. Instead he had him rolled in one of his own rugs and then had his cavalry ride back and forth over it, trampling him to death.

Justin Schmidt, a University of Arizona entomologist, has had himself bitten or stung by seventy-eight species of insect in order to rate them on a pain scale.

The custom of 'foot-binding' continued to be popular in China into the early twentieth century. The process consisted of wrapping the feet of young girls in tight bandages so that the feet would not develop normally. This binding caused four toes on each foot to break while the big toe remained intact. The bound feet would bend, becoming so concave that the woman developed a pitifully unsteady walk – something Chinese men found attractive; the smaller the foot, the more desirable the woman. The ideal foot was just was 3 inches (7.6 cm) long. The most common ailment of bound feet was infection. Toenails would grow sideways and could lead to flesh rotting, occasionally causing the toes to actually drop off. Disease inevitably followed infection and this sometimes led to death.

If you wanted to maximise your sexual pleasure you probably wouldn't think about injecting cocaine into your penis, but that's exactly what a thirty-four-year-old New Yorker decided to do. A very painful three-day-long erection was followed by blood clots forming in his penis, arms and legs. After twelve days in hospital he developed gangrene in all these appendages; his penis fell off when he was taking a bath and surgeons eventually had to amputate his legs and nine of his fingers.

American biologist Alfred Kinsey, author of *Sexual Behavior in the Human Male* (1948), could insert a toothbrush into his penis, bristle-end first.

The insane Emperor Nero had an inhumane but inventive way of providing illumination. He covered crucified Christians in tar and set them alight to form avenues of glowing torches that showed spectators the way to gladiatorial contests.

Lorena Bobbitt might have hit the news when she removed the penis of her wayward husband John, but Thai women have been doing this for years. In Thailand, penis attacks are more common than in any other country. In one case, a Thai woman threw the penis of her womanising husband out the window, where it was seized by a duck who waddled off with it dangling from its beak. In another instance, the spurned woman tied her husband's severed member to a bunch of helium balloons then released them into the air, never to be seen again (the penis or the balloons).

In the 1930s it was popular in the US to remove freckles by blasting the face with freezing carbon dioxide.

Trepanation (also known as trepanning) is surgery in which a hole is drilled into the human skull to expose the outermost layer of the brain. Nowadays the process is used for surgical access, but the technique was popular among many ancient civilisations to release evil spirits, or as a cure for madness or even migraines. Proponents also claim that exposing the brain in this way creates the 'third eye' and increases your consciousness in a similar way to an LSD trip. In 1970 a twenty-seven-year-old art student calmly recorded her DIY trepanation on camera. After the event she told a reporter that 'drilling a hole in one's head is really a nerve battle, doing something which obviously every instinct in your body is against. In a sense, it's quite satisfying that one can overcome one's nerves to do it.' The film, titled *Heartbeat in the Brain*, was shown in 1978 at the Suydam Gallery in New York. It was reported that, at the climax of the operation, several members of the audience fainted, 'dropping off their seats one by one like ripe plums'.

The Ottoman Sultan Osman II (who ruled 1618–1622) honed his archery skills by firing at live prisoners or pageboys.

The great Egyptologist Leonard Cottrell described the Ancient Egyptians as 'probably the most humane people of the ancient east'. Somebody obviously forgot to tell that to the nineteenth-dynasty pharaoh, Merneptah. He celebrated his victory over the Libyans at the city of Perire by cutting off their penises. A monument at Karnak records that his soldiers returned with a hoard of 13,240.

Someone with a similar idea was Queen Semiramis of Assyria. She took many lovers and was so jealous of the best that she took steps to make sure no other women would be able to experience what she did; she had their testicles removed.

A West Country man who was too impatient to wait for a sex change on the NHS decided to take matters into his own hands. In the privacy of his car, dressed in tights, high heels and a miniskirt, he severed his penis with a Stanley knife, and then threw it out of the window into a hedge. This act was observed by a passer-by, who rushed him to North Devon Hospital. The penis itself was retrieved by a farmer and packed in ice but authorities were reported as saying there were no plans to reunite it with its owner.

Victims of elephantiasis, a disease caused by the obstruction of lymph vessels due to parasitic filarial worms, can find their testicles swelling to the size of a watermelon – or larger. One of the worst cases on medical record involved an African whose scrotum weighed 154 lbs (70 kg) and measured almost 2 feet (61 cm) in diameter.

Forty-seven-year-old American Wesley Warren Jr's testicles suffered from scrotal lymphoedema, an infection of the lymph nodes which caused his testicles to swell to massive proportions and weigh almost 98 lbs (44 kg). A lengthy and highly specialised operation in April 2013 successfully removed the excess tissue and rebuilt Warren's scrotum.

The Turkish historian Abdi was selected by the Turkish Sultan Mehmed IV to write a running commentary of his reign. At the end of one day the Sultan asked Abdi what he'd written. Abdi replied that he hadn't written anything as nothing really important had happened. In response, Mehmed impaled the historian on his hunting spear, saying, 'Now you have something to write about.'

THE SPORTING LIFE

Aspiring Brazilian boxer Manuel Salgado, aged seventeen, suffered a huge blow – not to his head, but to his self-esteem and dignity – when his mother dragged him from the ring during a fight in Rio de Janeiro and ordered him to go home and finish his homework.

A sentry at a Greek air force base was a keen gymnast and liked to practise whenever he could. In February 1981 he was guarding a fleet of French Mirage fighter jets, which had stopped to refuel en route to Iraq. The long thin aerospike protruding from the nose cone of the nearest aircraft proved irresistible and, when no one was looking, he jumped up and began swinging on it, practising various gymnastic manoeuvres. To his horror, his weight bent the spike and he wasn't able to straighten it. There was only one thing to do... swing on the other three aircraft and recreate the bent spike so no one would notice. Except they did... and four new planes had to be flown out from France.

A squash ball moving at about 90 mph (145 km/h) has the same impact as a .22 bullet – and the ball can reach speeds of up to 170 mph (274 km/h).

The concept of the Olympic torch relay was a Nazi invention, devised to add spectacle to the 1936 Berlin Olympics.

Actor turned boxing commentator Michael Buffer not only coined the phrase 'Let's Get Ready to Rumble!' – he trademarked it. Since then he's earned an estimated $400 million by selling the rights to his phrase to movies, music, video games and other merchandise, and by making public appearances.

The Russian military rifle team proudly arrived at the 1908 Olympics in London, only to discover that the event had taken place several days earlier. It turned out that the Russians were using the old Julian calendar, oblivious to the fact that most of the world had adopted the faster-moving Gregorian.

Violent fighting broke out at a dominoes match in Sunderland in 1981 after it was discovered that one of the players was using pieces with removable dots.

The first recorded female golfer was Mary, Queen of Scots.

In what must have been one of the dullest ever boxing matches, in 1870, British boxing champion Jim Mace and American boxer Joe Coburn fought for three hours and forty-eight minutes without landing a single punch.

A new sport swept American universities in Massachusetts during 1939... live goldfish swallowing. In a short space of time it became an extremely competitive event, on a par with college football. Lothrop Withington Jr, a Harvard freshman, had eaten one for a $10 bet in March that year, a feat that was recorded by *The Boston Globe*. A few days later, Frank Hope of Marshall College in Pennsylvania called Withington a 'sissy' and swallowed three live goldfish. Harvard's pride was seriously dented but they retaliated when Irving Clark, another of their students, ate twenty-four live goldfish in five minutes. The race was well and truly on, with scores of campuses competing. Records tumbled daily throughout the spring, but within two months interest had worn off – though not before Clark University's Joseph Deliberato had devoured eighty-nine goldfish in one sitting. Psychologists have put the craze down to students wanting to release pre-exam tension. That, or because they 'took delight in the repulsiveness of the act'.

Despite its name, the Australian racehorse Bold Personality always finished well down the field, so when it did win a race in 1983 as a rank outsider, horse-racing officials were justifiably suspicious. All became clear after the race, when it became apparent that Bold Personality wasn't just dripping with sweat, it was dripping with emulsion. Its distinctive markings had been painted on; the 'ringer' was a much faster horse called Fine Cotton, which had been disguised by a gang of criminals running a betting scam in league with its trainers.

The 1900 Paris Olympics featured a live pigeon-shooting event. As its name implies, a flock of live birds were released in front of a participant with a shotgun. The contestant who killed the most birds won (if you really want to know, the gold medal winner was Léon de Lunden of Belgium, who killed twenty-one). Three hundred birds were killed during the event, but the sight of bloody feathers filling the air and maimed pigeons writhing on the ground caused the event to be dropped. Clay pigeons were used in the next Olympics.

Bill Cosby has a lifetime contract with the Harlem Globetrotters and gets paid $1.05 a year.

A three-hour baseball game contains about eighteen minutes of actual baseball action.

Greco-Roman wrestling was invented by a French solider, who so named it to give the impression it was played in ancient civilisations.

Trainer Piero Pucci coached a successful all-girl football team in Foggia, Italy, but faced a big problem just before a crucial cup match after his regular goalkeeper failed to turn up. With no substitutes good enough to take her place, Piero put on women's clothing and took to the field. Accessorising with a wig and a bra filled with two ripe watermelons, Piero performed admirably, even saving a penalty. His cover was blown, literally, in the second half when one of the watermelons exploded as he clashed with a striker. He was ordered off by the referee, who admitted later that he had found Piero 'attractive, in a homely sort of way'. When asked if he ever suspected that the goalkeeper was, in fact, a man, the ref said that Piero's hairy legs were 'not that unusual for a buxom country girl who had grown up in the hills tending sheep'.

At a cricket match that took place in Hong Kong in 1964, a ball was hit with so much force by a Mr Turner, captain of the Kowloon Cricket Club, that it split in two. Both halves went flying in different directions, and one was caught by a fielder. After due consideration and protests from both sides, the umpire declared the ball 'dead' and it was replayed.

Dr Renée Richards holds a unique achievement in sporting history. She competed in the US Open tennis championships as both a woman and a man (having competed initially as Richard Raskind).

It's a cliché when sportsmen say they feel as sick as a parrot, but Jim Kelly, quarterback for the Buffalo Bills, definitely was. Before each game he deliberately made himself vomit for good luck.

Paintball guns were originally invented as a way of marking cattle for slaughter.

Baseball legend Babe Ruth had a novel way to keep cool during hot games; he would put wet cabbage or lettuce leaves under his baseball cap. The same method was practised by top Korean pitcher Myung-Hwan Park, but the authorities intervened after cabbage leaves were seen to fall from his baseball cap during a televised game in 2005. After two hours' deliberation, the Korean Baseball Association ruled that cabbage was a 'foreign substance' and, as such, was banned from the field. However, they added that players could use cabbage in this way as long as they presented a doctor's note in advance.

Being short of a table tennis opponent didn't stop Ted Matson of Portland, Oregon, playing the game. His eight-year-old cat Dagwood would stand on the table and, with keen concentration, skilfully return the ball with her paw time after time. Known as the Ping Pong Pussy and the Table Tennis Tabby, Dagwood soon achieved celebrity status and appeared on the American *Movietone News* in 1962.

The spirit of 'backwardness' is celebrated each April Fool's Day in New York with a running backwards race, but running this way isn't as ridiculous as it sounds. Studies have shown it's a more efficient workout; one lap of backward running is the equivalent of four to six laps of forward running. Backward running also burns up to a third more calories than forward running and its gentler running style reduces the potential for injury.

MILITARY MATTERS

The German submarine U-1206 was reportedly sunk in 1945 as the direct result of a malfunctioning toilet.

At the peak of the 1991 Gulf War, British soldiers were issued with 500,000 sand-coloured condoms. These were not for leisure purposes but to keep the sand out of their gun barrels.

In World War Two the casualty rate among soldiers from venereal disease was often higher than actual battle casualties. In the 1943 Burma campaign battlefield casualties were thirteen per thousand men, while VD accounted for 157 victims per thousand.

Napoleon Bonaparte suffered from ailurophobia, a fear of cats.

During World War Two Geoffrey Pyke (cousin of TV boffin Dr Magnus Pyke) received the backing of the British and American high commands to develop his plan to tow large icebergs from the North Pole into the mid Atlantic where they could be used as mid-point fighter bases – in effect, huge ice aircraft carriers. Ice is unsinkable and it was known that icebergs, if large enough, would survive even in temperate waters. Encouraged by the government, Pyke's ambitions grew into creating massive 2-million-ton floating ice fortresses to take command of the whole of the North Atlantic. Leaving aside any misgivings about the actual sanity of the idea, colossal projected costs and practical difficulties killed off the notion.

NB Pyke always went around with his zip open, claiming this was for 'health reasons'.

Although an effective military leader before and during the Battle of Waterloo, Prussian field marshal Blücher had some increasingly irrational moments, a fact that was covered up by his staff. He would hop from foot to foot, believing that his servants, in the pay of the French, had made his floor too hot to stand on. He asked one servant to hit his head with a hammer after believing it had been turned to stone. He would also fight with imaginary people, breaking a lot of furniture in the process. One such bout of madness led him to admit to the Duke of Wellington, immediately after Waterloo, that he was pregnant with an elephant after being impregnated by a French guardsman.

Egyptian leader Muhammad Ali (1769–1849) had two infantry regiments that consisted solely of one-eyed soldiers.

It's a little-known fact that one mainland US location was bombed during World War Two. This was Boise City in Oklahoma – a victim of what today would be called 'friendly fire'.

The event took place at night on 5 July 1943 when a B-17 Flying Fortress bomber from nearby Dalhart Air Base mistook the lights surrounding the town square for a practice range. Bombs were dropped which caused damage to a church, a garage, a boarding house and the sidewalk, but fortunately there were no casualties.

The shortest war in history was fought between Britain and Zanzibar in 1896. It was over in thirty-eight minutes and Zanzibar's only warship, the HHS *Glasgow*, was sunk after just fifteen minutes of open fire.

In 2008 the Pentagon spent more money every five seconds in Iraq than the average American earned in a year.

Benito Mussolini so wanted to impress Hitler that he lied frequently about the size of the Italian air force – eventually believing his own tales. The true figure was about four hundred bombers and a hundred fighter aircraft, but Mussolini had convinced the Führer (and himself) that there was a total of 8,530 aircraft. When Mussolini announced a nationwide inspection of his air force, Air Ministry officials, in order to avoid punishment or execution, arranged to have entire squadrons flown from airfield to airfield ahead of him where they could be counted again and again. Mussolini, and Hitler, never discovered the truth.

For every hour the B2 bomber spends in the air, it needs twenty-four hours of maintenance on the ground.

Private Henry Tandey was a highly decorated soldier in World War One and, although he was awarded the VC, DCM and Military Medal, is perhaps better known as the man who could have killed Hitler... but didn't. It happened in September 1918 during a fierce battle in the French village of Marcoing. During the conflict a bedraggled, wounded German corporal staggered out in front of Tandey, who raised his rifle and took aim. Tandey later said that, after staring at each other for a considerable length of time, he couldn't bring himself to kill the unarmed man and lowered his gun. The two men nodded at each other and the German limped away. Tandey recognised Hitler during his later rise to power as the man he had let go. At the height of the Blitz, twenty-two years later, Tandey publicly regretted not pulling the trigger, saying, 'If only I had known what he would turn out to be.'

In 2005 the US press got hold of leaked documents that referred to experiments conducted by the US Air Force Research Laboratory. These studies, carried out at Wright-Patterson Air Force Base in Ohio, related to the development of non-lethal combat weapons. Among those proposed were biological weapons to cause body odour and flatulence among enemy troops, creating embarrassment and lack of morale, and a powerful aphrodisiac that might cause enemy soldiers to lay down their arms and embrace their fellow man. None of these weapons were developed. Apparently.

Vikings about to go to war would try to ensure they had luck on their side. They would bind prisoners to the wooden rollers that launched their ships, believing that human blood smeared along the keels would bring victory.

During World War Two a Pennsylvania dentist developed an innovative secret weapon: a miniature incendiary bomb that could be strapped to a bat's body and then dropped over Japan. The thinking behind this was that the bats would land in the country's wooden homes and buildings and would soon chew through the string that held the bombs to their bodies, causing the bombs to fall and explode. After convincing the White House of his plan, the first tests went ahead in New Mexico in 1943, but these were not a success. The bats landed in the wrong places and set fire to the barracks and control tower of a brand new and as yet unoccupied air force base, as well as setting alight a general's staff car. Two million dollars and thirty tests later, the project was eventually abandoned.

Genghis Khan's Mongol horde didn't wash for two reasons. Firstly, the thick crust of dirt on their skin was thought to have provided protection against the extreme cold. Secondly, their lack of hygiene was believed to give them a psychological advantage; apparently their enemies would be paralysed with fear, smelling the army approaching long before they saw it.

The Royal Flying Corps was reluctant to issue any of its airmen parachutes at the start of World War One. There was a feeling among some of the flying establishment that the use of parachutes was a bit 'unmanly'.

The US Army once issued this sage advice to avoid typhoid: 'All ice cubes will be boiled before use.'

The Russian Czar Paul I was obsessed with the appearance of his army, putting the way they looked above any regard for military effectiveness. To avoid creases, their uniforms were so tight-fitting that any form of combat would have been impossible. Under their uniforms the soldiers wore straitjackets and had steel plates strapped to their knees to maintain their posture while marching.

WEIRD LEADERS

King John V of Portugal, the aptly nicknamed 'John the Magnanimous', combined his interests in sex and Catholicism by regularly sleeping with nuns.

It's widely believed that King Henry VIII liked roast beef so much that he officially knighted it, a possible origin of the word 'sirloin', as in 'Arise, Sir Loin!'

King Henry III of France, who ruled 1574–1589, was known as 'The Transvestite King'. He would often attend court functions in full drag and was known to carry a basket of small dogs.

When Peter the Great (1682–1725), the Czar of Russia, came to England to study shipbuilding in 1698, he once got so drunk that he asked his friends to push him through a holly bush in a wheelbarrow.

William, Duke of Normandy, was illegitimate and soon acquired the nickname William the Bastard. It's said that he quietly simmered with anger every time he heard that name, but what upset him even more was being known as the son of a tanner, a reference to his mother Herleva, who was the daughter of a common leather tanner. Assisting King Henry I of France in his war against a rebellious count during 1048–1049, William laid siege to the city of Alençon. To goad their attacker, some more daring members of the population hung hides from the city walls to remind William of his mother's lowly heritage. William is reported to have sworn that when he took the city he would cut off the hands of those who'd mocked him. As good as his word, William was victorious and thirty-two city leaders had their hands cut off. After his success at the Battle of Hastings seventeen years later and his subsequent coronation, the duke acquired a new nickname that would stick with him: William the Conqueror.

Adolf Hitler was declared *Time* magazine's 'Man of the Year 1938'.

US President James A. Garfield could simultaneously write Latin with one hand and Greek with the other.

During the tenth century, the Grand Vizier of Persia insisted on transporting his entire library wherever he went. This consisted of 117,000 volumes and was split among a procession of four hundred camels, which were trained to walk in alphabetical order.

King Louis XIV is said to have only taken three baths in his entire life, each of them under protest, while diarist Samuel Pepys is said to have never taken a bath.

Caligula, who ruled AD 37–41, is known as one of the maddest of all the Roman emperors. One of his favourite methods of torture was covering his enemies with honey and setting an army of red wasps loose on them. He was eventually stabbed to death by the most devoted member of his Praetorian Guard, after he had made the burly soldier dress up in women's clothing and act like he was a prostitute.

The Queen owns all dolphins, porpoises and sturgeons in British waters.

Former Vietnamese leader Ho Chi Minh once worked as a dishwasher at the Drayton Court Hotel in west London.

After Napoleon died in exile in 1821, it was reported that his body did not receive the respect many felt was due to such an imperial leader. His teeth were said to have been pulled out by an Irish doctor and sold for ten guineas each, and most of his internal organs were said to have been stolen by doctors present at the autopsy. His heart was allegedly taken by an English doctor, who left it in a sink overnight for safe keeping, where it was subsequently meant to have been eaten by rats. His intestines were found in a jar at the British Royal College of Surgeons but were subsequently destroyed in a German air raid in 1940. But possibly his greatest indignity was the removal of his penis by his priest-confessor. Passing through the hands of various collectors, the penis was displayed on a small velvet cushion in New York's Museum of French Art, where it was described as looking like a 'shrivelled eel'. It was bought for $3,000 in 1977 by an eminent American doctor, who added it to his collection of the weird and wonderful that also included Abraham Lincoln's bloodstained collar from the night of his assassination and pieces of the car in which John F. Kennedy was shot.

Winston Churchill started smoking cigars aged fifteen.

Saparmurat Atayevich Niyazov was president of Turkmenistan from 1990 to 2006 and created a cult of personality by erecting statues of solid gold in his honour, establishing a national holiday to celebrate his birthday, and using his control of the media to praise him daily. His egomania reached a peak when he changed the calendar and renamed days of the week and months after Turkmenistan heroes, members of his own family and, of course, himself.

Queen Victoria was prescribed marijuana by her physician to relieve her menstrual cramps.

King Farouk of Egypt was known as a funny and charming man, yet one with some very bizarre quirks. He was a glutton who was also addicted to fizzy drinks, drinking at least thirty a day. Also impulsive, he once suffered a series of nightmares about lions, so his solution to make the dreams stop was to go to Cairo Zoo and shoot its lions in their cage (the nightmares continued). Car mad, Farouk owned more than a hundred vehicles, all of which were sprayed red – and he forbade anyone in Egypt to own another red vehicle. Although he was immensely wealthy, Farouk was a kleptomaniac and even took pickpocket lessons from a professional thief. At official receptions and parties, Farouk would steal watches, wallets and cigarette lighters; on one occasion he even stole Winston Churchill's pocket watch. He was also an avid collector – but of really trivial items such as matchboxes, razorblades and toothpaste tubes.

George Washington had to borrow money to travel to his own presidential inauguration.

Empress Wu of China demanded that all visiting dignitaries must pay their respects by 'the licking of the lotus stamen'. She was depicted in many portraits lifting her gown to various statesmen to allow unhindered access to her genitals. This practice of imperial cunnilingus has since been discontinued.

Attila the Hun is reported to have died from a nosebleed during a banquet.

Peter the Great did not take too kindly to the fact that his favourite mistress, the beautiful and witty Mary Hamilton, had been unfaithful to him. He had her beheaded and, although there exist conflicting stories, it was said that he kept her head pickled in a large jar of alcohol in his bedroom as a warning to subsequent lovers.

Adolf Hitler's favourite film was *King Kong*, while Stalin was a fan of the Tarzan films.

Saddam Hussein's two favourite films were *Enemy of the State* and *Day of the Jackal*.

The tomb of King Richard I at Westminster Abbey used to have a hole in it so that visitors could reach inside and touch his skull.

No one knows for certain precisely what triggered King George III of England's bouts of madness; it was probably a combination of factors, including an inherited rare blood disorder called porphyria, mental illness and dementia. Stories abound about his irrational behaviour, such as him yelling at courtiers that London was under water, or talking non-stop for nineteen hours, his conversation punctuated with crude sexual innuendo. Other reports claim he insisted on saying the word 'peacock!' at the end of every sentence, or would often wear a pillowcase on his head. Sometimes, believing that he was dead, he would wear black and announce that he was mourning for 'that great man, King George'. It was also reported that once, while riding in his coach through Windsor Great Park, the king suddenly ordered his driver to stop. He then jumped out of the coach, walked over to an oak tree, shook hands with one of its branches and talked to it for several minutes. The king thought that he had been addressing the King of Prussia.

George III, however, was far from being the only 'mad royal':

/ King Charles VI of France was insane for most of his forty-two-year rule and was convinced that his legs were made of glass. He refused to travel by coach in case his legs shattered.

- King Otto of Bavaria's mental illness manifested itself by him barking like a dog, yelling abuse at his courtiers, and shooting from his window at anyone unfortunate enough to be passing by.

- Philip, the eldest son of Charles III of Spain, had a fixation about gloves and was said to have worn sixteen pairs at the same time.

- The Russian Grand Duke Constantine liked to while away the hours shooting live rats out of a cannon.

- The Hapsburg Emperor Ferdinand I was said to climb into a large waste-paper bin and roll around the floor in it, and also to chase flies around the palace and try to catch them with his hands. One of his oddest royal edicts was when he supposedly declared to his court, 'I'm the Emperor and I want dumplings.'

Some believe it's a myth but stories claim that the prematurely born and very weak Kaiser Leopold I of Austria was regularly wrapped or dunked in the carcass of a freshly slaughtered pig in order to help him gain strength. This meat was subsequently given to the poor, who called it 'Kaiserfleisch'.

Even among Roman emperors Elagabalus achieved notoriety for his levels of eccentricity and debauchery; one of his biographers described him as having an 'unspeakably disgusting life'. Elagabalus was known to cross-dress and wear make-up, then prostitute himself in taverns. He would also stand naked in the doorway of his bedroom in the Imperial Palace and make advances at passers-by, even members of his elite guard. He was fascinated with the idea of castration and spoke endlessly about the best techniques. Although he didn't go this far himself, he did have himself circumcised and forced members of the senate to watch. His banquets redefined excess; at one dinner he served the brains of 600 ostriches while he had a penchant for the tongues of peacocks and nightingales, believing this would make him immune from the plague. Although he lived a life of extreme decadence, it was a short one. He was assassinated, aged eighteen, by his guards, who'd grown weary of his depravity.

WHAT A WAY TO GO...

The Athenian legislator Draco designed an early legal code that was, needless to say, draconian. In spite of this he was very popular with the citizens of Athens who, in 590 BC, held a testimonial in his honour at the theatre of Aegina. As Draco entered the arena thousands of well-wishers showed their appreciation in the customary way – by showering him with their hats, shirts and cloaks; Draco suffocated to death in the pile of clothing and was buried in the theatre.

Cornishman Bobby Leach, the first man to go over Niagara Falls in a barrel (he was the second person to do so because an American woman had beaten him to it), died after slipping on an orange peel while on a publicity tour in New Zealand.

French ornithologist Marius Giraud spent hundreds of hours at home perfecting his bird calls. After he was satisfied, he went into some nearby woods to try them out – and was almost immediately shot dead by a hunter.

At a stag party in Cosenza, Italy, in August 1997, guests were curious and somewhat annoyed when a stripper they'd hired to leap out of a giant cake failed to make her appearance. Assuming she was no longer in there, they later received a nasty shock when they found her dead inside it. The stripper had suffocated after waiting for an hour inside the sealed cake.

In 1993 an Icelandic funeral parlour was fined after the family of Henri Labonte discovered that the deceased had been dressed by the undertakers for his 26 December funeral wearing a Santa Claus outfit and fake bushy white beard.

The inventor of the iconic Pringles can, Fredric J. Baur, died in an Ohio hospice in May 2008 just a few days before his ninetieth birthday. In keeping with his wishes, his body was cremated and his ashes placed in a Pringles can which was then buried. His children said that their father was so proud of the tube-shaped container he patented in 1970 that he wanted one to accompany him to his grave. (If you're interested, the can was Original flavour.)

Just three months after he died on Christmas Day 1977, Charlie Chaplin's body was dug up from his grave in Vevey, Switzerland, by two unemployed immigrants who thought they could hold the body ransom and extort money from his widow Oona. After she refused to pay, they threatened Chaplin's youngest children with violence and were eventually caught in a police operation in March 1978. Chaplin's body was recovered and buried a second time, this time under 6 feet of reinforced concrete.

Funerals in the Tana Toraja region of Indonesia are grand events accompanied by music, dance and a feast for a large number of mourners – and are therefore expensive affairs. To enable the family to save for the funeral, the body does not have to be buried right away. Instead it's preserved, wrapped and taken to the family home where it can be kept for weeks, months or even years until there is enough money for the ceremony. Until the actual burial, the corpse is treated as a sick person and is included in daily conversations.

The Pashtun tribes of Afghanistan are infamous for having one of the most bizarre and cruel ways to execute someone... drowning the victim in urine. Last recorded in 1933, the method involved pegging the victim out and, with a stick, forcing his jaws wide open so he could not swallow. The tribeswomen would then take it in turns to squat and urinate into the victim's mouth until he died.

An eighteen-stone man was trying to hang himself from an aqueduct over the River Ouse in North Yorkshire in February 1986 when the rope broke. He drowned instead.

In 1988 two New York lawyers raced each other down one of the longest corridors in their office. One of the lawyers failed to stop and continued out of a thirty-ninth-floor window.

A man tried to commit suicide by jumping off the roof of the Chinese embassy in London. Having climbed up there, he decided that life was worth living after all and started to make his way back down. On his descent he slipped and fell 40 feet to his death.

Sunee Whitworth and her friend Anuban Bell were killed by a bolt of lightning after the metal in one of their underwired bras acted as a conductor. The women were sheltering under a tree during a thunderstorm in London's Hyde Park in October 1999 when they were electrocuted. The Westminster coroner recorded a verdict of death by misadventure.

When Dallas police discovered the badly mutilated remains of a woman in a garage in 1981, they questioned the house's owner Orvell Wyatt Lloyd. He admitted killing his mother-in-law but said he'd mistaken her for a large racoon when he hacked her to death.

Prisoners being held in a jail in Belo Horizonte, Brazil, decided that they needed to make a real impact in their protest against overcrowding. They decided that two prisoners should die in an effort to draw attention to the conditions, and promptly held a lottery to decide who would be sacrificed for the greater good. The two unlucky 'winners' were then punched and kicked to death by the other inmates.

A Los Angeles drug addict with a long history of mental illness killed himself after digging a large hole in his garden and burying himself alive. His mother later told police that her son had delusions that he was a mole.

In May 1987 a sixty-one-year-old Nottinghamshire man killed himself by hammering two 5-inch nails into his skull. The coroner stated that he believed this was the first recorded case of this method of suicide.

In 1983 Tony Gribble of Bristol made a request to be cremated and his ashes placed in an egg timer, so he could continue to be of use to his family after his death.

Mrs Martha Metcalfe was buried in Blairsville, Georgia, in July 1982. The preacher was finishing his eulogy by uttering the words, 'And we never know what is going to happen next', when a bolt of lightning hit the mourners standing at the graveside, killing her grandson Donald. Other members of the family suffered burns.

It could only happen in the gambling capital of the world... Staff in the intensive care ward of a Las Vegas hospital were suspended in March 1980 after it was discovered they'd been betting on when critically ill patients would die. Police were called after hospital officials suspected that some patients' oxygen supplies had been tampered with in order to win wagers.

An engineer died at Delhi airport after being accidentally sucked into the engine of a Boeing 737. The cause of death was reported as 'shock'.

In October 1973, in accordance with his wishes, Roland Ohisson, a Swedish confectionery salesman, was buried in a coffin made entirely of chocolate.

YES, BUT IS IT ART?

On arrival at London's Tate Gallery in 1985, visitors were pleased and critically positive to see an unannounced avant-garde art installation. Museum staff didn't have the heart to tell them it was actually 280 art students protesting against education budget cuts.

The Cure for Insomnia, a movie released in January 1987, runs for 5,220 minutes (87 hours, or just over three and a half days). By filmmaker/artist/musician John Timmis IV, the film mainly consists of poet L. D. Groban reading poetry, spliced with X-rated film clips and heavy metal rock videos.

Samuel Beckett's play *Breath* was first performed in October 1969. It lasts thirty seconds and consists of off-stage birth cries and heavy breathing.

Leonardo da Vinci never signed or dated any of his work, not even his most famous painting, the *Mona Lisa*.

Authors have some very strange habits: Goethe liked to write with rotten apples decomposing in his desk drawer; James Joyce preferred to write with a large blue pencil while lying on his stomach in bed; Truman Capote often wrote lying down and wouldn't begin or end a piece of work on a Friday; it's said that Ernest Hemingway wrote all his books while eating just peanut butter sandwiches; and, in order to make sure he completed *The Hunchback of Notre Dame* on deadline, Victor Hugo had all his clothes locked away so he wouldn't be tempted to leave his house.

One of the themes running through the work of the late French-Canadian feminist sculptor Louise Bourgeois was testicles. Her piece *No Exit* is a stairway with two huge testicles preventing anyone from leaving, while *Untitled with Foot* consists of a baby being crushed by a massive testicle.

The American artist Keith Boadwee has rather a novel name for his individual technique. He calls it 'butthole painting'. Using enema bags, he injects himself full of water-based paint, which he then evacuates over a canvas while naked. His art has been described as both 'poignant' and 'bad ass', and his paintings have been compared to some of the best works of Jackson Pollock.

In 2007 Cypriot-Australian performance artist Stelarc had a cell-cultivated human ear surgically attached to his left arm.

In 1994 the Esbjerg Art Gallery in Denmark displayed an exhibit by Christian Lemmerz consisting of a large glass tank containing the bodies of six recently killed pigs. Visitors would watch them decompose and change in colour from pink to black. The artist announced this exhibit was for those who valued reality in art.

French entertainer Michel Lotito went by the stage name of Monsieur Mangetout and ate anything he fancied. Meals included ten bicycles, 400 metres of steel chain, a pair of skis, a full-size brass-handled coffin, numerous TV sets and computers, some supermarket trolleys and even an entire Cessna 150 light aircraft. When performing, he would eat around 1 kg of materials daily, lubricating them with mineral oil and drinking considerable quantities of water. He died in 2007, aged fifty-seven, from natural causes.

Artist William Turnbull won the second prize of £3,000 at the John Moores art exhibition in Liverpool in 1978. His work called *Untitled No. 9* was a canvas that had been painted completely white. The artist explained that he'd written 'Top' on the back on two different sides, because his work could be hung either way since it was 'not gravitationally oriented'.

In 1981 the British Arts Council paid £7,000 for a work from two Norfolk artists that mainly consisted of old horseshoes, decaying leaves, an old Wellington boot and carefully arranged horse manure and rabbit droppings. The work was exhibited at the Serpentine Gallery. Comments in the visitors' book ranged from 'oversimplified' to 'bullshit'.

The *Mona Lisa* was stolen from the Louvre in 1911 but it was twenty-four hours before anyone even noticed it had been taken. The portrait was missing for two years before it was recovered, during which time more people came to stare at the blank space on the wall where it had once hung than had actually been to look at the masterpiece itself.

An exhibition by contemporary Swedish artist Goran Hagg at the Pompidou Centre in Paris in 1981 consisted of a model of a bare-chested woman that spat water at visitors. The catalogue stated that the piece posed 'intricate questions pertaining to the relationship of art and reality'.

In 1982 the Scottish National Gallery of Modern Art paid £23,000 for a work by French sculptor César Baldaccini entitled *Compression 1966*; a 162 cm x 68 cm x 66 cm (64 in x 27 in x 26 in) 'cube' made of crushed car parts. A local scrap merchant offered to create the same work for £6.

When the Venice *Carnevale* was reintroduced in 1979, local mask-maker Giorgio Spiller protested against the commerciality of the reborn event by dressing up as a giant penis, a costume that was described as being 'beautifully constructed and manifestly grotesque'. He was arrested for offending public decency, but his defence lawyer drew upon the previous year's festival where no charges had been brought against him despite him dressing up that time as a giant vagina.

Luminaries of the British art scene, Gilbert and George, have included images of excrement in their art as far back as 1983 with their work *Shitted*. In 1994 they created *The Naked Shit Pictures*, in which they appear naked alongside giant turds. Commenting on their work, the artists have said, 'Fundamentally there's something religious about the fact that we're made from shit.'

In the 1890s American showman Tommy Minnock toured New Jersey theatres with a novel act; he allowed himself to be crucified on stage. While volunteers drove nails into his hands and feet he would sing 'After The Ball Is Over'.

In 1961 Italian artist Piero Manzoni packed his faeces in tin cans, which he then signed and sold as art.

A Parable of the Blind at the Edinburgh Festival in 1988 was billed as: 'Blind, blissful, medieval figures dance towards Brueghel's inevitable ditch, while in a mythical East, goldfish have their eyes plucked out in order to sing better.' No one showed up.

There is a Hair Museum in Independence, Missouri, which contains over two thousand exhibits of 'hair art', pieces containing or made from human hair. Exhibits include wreaths, watch fobs, bracelets, necklaces, earrings, chains, brooches, hatpins, postcards and pictures.

It's a great achievement when your play opens on Broadway, but it's not so good when it closes the same night. That happened to *Moose Murders* by Arthur Bicknell, a work considered by many to be the worst play ever performed on Broadway. This 'musical mystery farce' took place one stormy night in Wild Moose Lodge, where the characters thrown together included a man in a moose costume, a janitor who looked like a native American but who talked with an Irish brogue, a Nazi-like nurse, a blind organist, a drug-crazed hippy and a bandage-wrapped quadriplegic. The plot was even more confusing. After it opened and closed on 22 February 1983, the celebrated *New York Times* critic Frank Rich commented, 'From now on there will always be two groups of theatregoers in the world. Those who have seen *Moose Murders* and those who have not. Those of us who have witnessed it will undoubtedly hold periodic reunions in the noble tradition of the survivors of the *Titanic*.'

Children from China's Sichuan province, with a little help from famous sculptor Zhu Cheng, created a replica of the *Venus de Milo* out of giant panda dung.

Mozart wrote a canon in B-flat major titled 'Leck mich im Arsch', which translates as 'Lick me in the arse'.

JUST PLAIN WEIRD

Ed Gein, a middle-aged man from Wisconsin, was the inspiration for the films *Psycho* and *Silence of the Lambs*. Gein was a necrophiliac who started by digging up female corpses, before turning to murder. A police raid in 1957 found the following items in his fridge: bracelets made of human skin, two lips on a string, four noses in a cup and dozens of human organs.

In New Carrollton, Maryland, just on the outskirts of Washington DC, there's a Museum of Menstruation. Located in the basement of a suburban house, it was established as a way of educating people about this taboo subject and, in the words of its founder and curator, Harry Finley, 'it combines anthropology, sociology, history and art.' The museum's popularity and associated safety concerns have meant that general admissions have now ceased and, until Harry finds a new public location, it's currently open to the public by appointment only.

Swastika is a town in Northern Ontario, Canada, that grew up around a gold-mining site in 1908. During World War Two the provincial government wanted to change the town's name to Winston in honour of the British prime minster but the town refused, citing the fact that it had held the name long before the Germans had adopted the symbol of the same name. Weirdly, though, the notorious British Nazi-sympathiser Unity Mitford was conceived in Swastika, where her family owned a gold mine.

Only certain Asian people have genuinely black hair. Every other 'black' hair colour is actually a very dark brown.

The rights to the computer game *Tetris* were originally owned by the Soviet Union. The inventor, Alexey Pajitnov, worked for the Dorodnicyn Computing Centre, which was part of the Soviet Academy of Sciences. Since Pajitnov was working for the Soviet government at the time and using their equipment, they retained the rights to the game and the royalties. After the Soviet Union was dissolved in 1991 Pajitnov moved to the US. Finally, in 1996, the rights were passed to him and he finally started earning royalties for the game he had invented twelve years previously.

Every time you lick a stamp, you consume one-tenth of a calorie.

A judge in Kansas City refused permission for a local Greek man to change his name from Evans as his intended name would be too long for computers to deal with. He'd wanted to call himself Xartheohadjimadurokaszamnoupoulis.

The most remote cash machine is located at McMurdo Station, an American Antarctic research centre. The ATM is maintained by the Wells Fargo banking group, which installed two machines – not because long queues are a problem on the base, but as a precaution in case one stops working; maintenance is performed only once every two years.

In 2007 Liu Ye, a thirty-nine-year-old Chinese man, married someone very close – himself. The surreal wedding ceremony involved Liu Ye marrying a life-size cardboard cut-out of himself, dressed for the occasion in a red silk dress. The groom, who admitted to being 'a little bit narcissistic', then paraded his new cardboard spouse around the wedding banquet for the traditional business of greeting and toasting the guests.

A survey showed that most British people are happiest at 7.26 on a Saturday night.

Who would have thought there are so many 'types' of tiny paper discs left behind by a hole punch? Generally known as 'chad', this waste product is usually quite innocuous, but 'hanging', 'dimpled' and even 'pregnant' chad were all blamed for an abundance of votes going uncounted in the punchcard voting system used in the 2000 presidential ballot in Florida.

Talk show host Johnny Carson caused a national toilet paper shortage in December 1973 by a throwaway jokey remark he made on *The Tonight Show*. He happened to say, 'You know what's disappearing from the supermarket shelves? Toilet paper... there's an acute shortage of toilet paper in the United States.' Of course, there wasn't, but the population panicked and bought up and hoarded as much as they could. Supermarkets tried to ration it but by noon the next day, most of the nation's supermarkets had sold out. After several days of toilet paper shortage Carson went on air to apologise for the joke and the hysteria that it had caused; the shortage lasted for almost a month.

The Guinness Book of Records holds the record for being the book most often stolen from public libraries.

A merkin is a pubic wig – an accessory that's had many uses throughout history. In Elizabethan theatre it was used as an obvious prop when boys and men played female roles. Because one of the old treatments for syphilis involved shaving off pubic hair, women turned to merkins to improve their appearance (as they concealed their syphilitic sores). In pre-war America it was illegal to strip completely nude, so wearing a merkin was an effective defence against any public decency charges.

The sum of all the numbers on a roulette wheel is 666.

Described by MTV as 'the weirdest magazine in the world', *Girls and Corpses* brings together two very diverse interests: beautiful girls and decaying corpses. According to its publisher, it's 'sort of like *Maxim* magazine meets *Dawn of the Dead*'.

Transport minister Ephraem Magagula had to admit to the Swaziland parliament that the landlocked country had lost track of its only naval warship, the *Swazimar*. Denying any incompetence on behalf of the government, parliament was reassured by the minister that 'the situation was absolutely under control'. He emphasised that 'the Swazimar is a big ship painted in the sort of nice bright colours you can see at night. Mark my words, it will turn up.'

The national anthem of Greece contains 158 verses.

Modelled on green extremists in Australia known as 'ferals', Feral Cheryl was designed as a Barbie doll for 'alternative lifestylers'. She has dreadlocks, pierced nipples, a range of tattoos and pubic hair. Company spokesperson Leigh Duncan commented, 'There have been written complaints and I received some death threats because of Feral's range of accessories, including recycled tampons that can be inserted and removed, and an imitation bag of marijuana. Ferals don't relate to the clean Barbie image. Cheryl is a slut and that's that.'

The official name for the hash symbol # is the octothorpe.

Early advertisements for Coca-Cola's bottled water Dasani called it 'bottled spunk' and featured the slogan 'Can't live without spunk'. Coca-Cola seemed initially oblivious to the slang meaning of 'spunk' in the UK and the ads were soon dropped.

There's a social club in America that goes by the snappy acronym of ATDPFCTJ... or, as it's better known, the Association To Deter People From Calling Toilets John. It's open to anyone who has John as their first, middle or last name and they campaign tirelessly to prevent their name being sullied by any connection to the loo.

A third-century medical book describes how the magic word 'Abracadabra' was used to ward off malaria.

The Electro-Bash, held in South Pasadena, California, allows people suffering from what's known as Consumer Electronics Stress Syndrome to vent their frustrations. Events include the 'Slam Dunk', where participants heave recalcitrant electronic devices off a balcony, and the 'Sledge-O-Matic', where they don protective glasses and wield a sledgehammer to smash their least-favourite electronic gadgets, devices and appliances.

There's only one British place name that ends with an exclamation mark: Westward Ho!

Some of the weirdest items for sale have been found on eBay, including: a pint of sun-dried California yellowjacket bees; a plucked nipple hair with purported medicinal properties; a face found in a chocolate chip cookie; a 'mutant cucumber' (described as perishable); an F/A-18 Hornet fighter jet (which didn't achieve its $1 million sale price); a whole town (Bridgeville, California: population 25); an unwanted Christmas dinner Brussels sprout; a single cornflake; and water from a plastic cup that Elvis Presley reportedly drank from. In May 2006 a man from Brisbane attempted to sell New Zealand with bidding starting at just one Australian cent. The price had risen to A$3,000 before eBay pulled the auction.

WANKSY

INTERPRETING A GRAFFITI VIRTUOSO

PARENTAL ADVISORY EXPLICIT CONTENT

MARC BLAKEWILL
& JAMES HARRIS

WANKSY
Interpreting a Graffiti Virtuoso

Marc Blakewill & James Harris

£9.99

Hardback

ISBN: 978-1-84953-474-1

Wanksy is the unheralded genius behind some of the most iconic urban images of our time: the seminal 'cock and balls', the timeless 'Leroy loves Sarah', the devastatingly direct 'sod' and countless other masterpieces. For the first time, this book collects Wanksy's most significant works to date, together with expert critiques that analyse and illuminate their hidden depths. You'll never look at a crudely drawn penis in the same way again.

OMG

Short for 'Oh my God!', used to express surprise at events ranging from nuclear blasts to lost socks.

OMG

£4.99

Hardback

ISBN: 978-1-84953-487-1

Whether you're one of the Twitterati or someone who thinks tweeting is something birds do, you've probably heard people saying 'OMG!' to each other (after all, we're too darned busy for 'Oh my God' nowadays). This little book will introduce you to an unrivalled selection of amazing facts, along with playful #hashtag commentaries – dive in and you'll be OMG-ing before you know it! #wellinever

YOLO

Abbreviation for 'you only live once' – handy way of saying 'carpe diem' for people who don't speak Latin.

YOLO

£4.99

Hardback

ISBN: 978-1-84953-489-5

It is a truth universally acknowledged that You Only Live Once, so while some of us have been using the words 'Carpe diem!' or 'Seize the day!', it would be far more economical just to shout 'YOLO!' This little book brings together a selection of fascinating facts accompanied by inspiring #hashtags to stir you into action. You'll soon be seizing the day so firmly it'll be begging for mercy. #ouchletgo

Have you enjoyed this book?
If so, why not write a review on your favourite website?

If you're interested in finding out more about our
books, find us on Facebook at **Summersdale Publishers**
and follow us on Twitter at **@Summersdale**.

Thanks very much for buying this Summersdale book.

www.summersdale.com